CONNECTING

**A HANDBOOK FOR HOUSEWIVES
RETURNING TO PAID WORK**

CONNECTING

A HANDBOOK FOR HOUSEWIVES
RETURNING TO PAID WORK

SALLY ASHLEY

82 8178-10

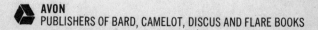
AVON
PUBLISHERS OF BARD, CAMELOT, DISCUS AND FLARE BOOKS

For my family — and especially for

PETER

PEGGY

CAREY

TOM

and

DAVID.

CONNECTING: A HANDBOOK FOR HOUSEWIVES RETURNING TO PAID WORK is an original publication of Avon Books. This work has never before appeared in book form.

AVON BOOKS
A division of
The Hearst Corporation
959 Eighth Avenue
New York, New York 10019

Copyright © 1982 by Sally Ashley
Published by arrangement with the author
Library of Congress Catalog Card Number: 80-69888
ISBN: 0-380-79251-6

Book design by Sheldon Winicour

Library of Congress Cataloging in Publication Data

Ashley, Sally.
   Connecting: a handbook for housewives returning to
paid work.

   1. Vocational guidance for women.   2. Housewives—
Employment.   I. Title.
HF5381.A832   650.1′4′024042   80-69888
ISBN 0-380-79251-6   AACR2

First Avon Printing, May, 1982

DON   10 9 8 7 6 5 4 3 2 1

Contents

2159315

PART ONE

A Case History: My Own Story

CHAPTER ONE

Forty Years
Before the Mast

IN ORDER TO PERSUADE MY FRENCH TEACHER TO award me the D minus which would enable me to graduate from high school, I had to promise him I would never take French again as long as I lived, and if, by some catastrophic necessity, I ever did, I was not to mention him. I have kept my side of the bargain without difficulty and now, twenty-eight years later, feel it permissible at last to announce his name. Greetings to you, Mr. Donald Fontaine, wherever you are. I apologize to you for the ulcers I must have given you and I forgive you the heartache you caused me.

Besides being a blatant underachiever (oh, happy euphemism), I was also among the most single-minded of the thirty-eight students in that class of 1952 at Ottawa Hills, in Toledo, Ohio. From the age of eleven I was desperate to get married and during high school the obsession became teeth-gritting strong.

I suspect one of the reasons for my dismal social life during that time (my big brother secretly paid a younger fellow five dollars and expenses to take me to the Senior Prom—though not secretly enough, as it turned out) was the very strength and tenacity of my determination. Surely there is an identifiable mad look in a matrimony-crazed girl's eyes warning off even the most sex-starved teen-age boy. The look says, "I want to be a *wife*."

When I did marry, in 1956, I had four children in four and a half years, perhaps to remind myself I had caught a husband and my life was legitimate, after all. Clearly I was a conventional young woman who had grown up with one foot in the last century. For most of the preceding twenty-one years I had hungered for the marriage ritual of passage but I was prepared for nothing further afterwards. The future was obscured by a rosy cloud cover as I stood on its threshold.

Twenty-one years later, I am president of a small company, run workshops and counseling sessions, meet with representatives of "top management," talk on the radio and wait around in airports. I am no longer married, my children are pretty well launched into the world, and there is dust collecting on the on–off switch of my vacuum cleaner.

As it turns out, I am the first woman in the direct line of my female antecedents to be divorced, to run a business, to earn a graduate degree, to have my own accountant. These are remarkable facts when you think that there were several thousand generations of females preceding me in the continuum and, as far as I know, not one of them did what I'm doing.

Recently my mother told me "the man in the bookstore" had offered her a job when she was around my age (forty-six). I'm sure she would have been a fine salesperson—her love for books is effervescent and contagious—but she talked the possibility over with my father and they decided she should turn down the job offer. Dad was traveling a lot and, since all of us kids were finally grown up, she could at last accompany him. It was something they'd waited for for a long time, so Mom said "no." I have no opinion on the merit of the decision, yet the story fascinates me because it was the only job my mother was ever offered and she remembered it clearly twenty-five years afterwards. There is something terrific about being paid for what you do, no matter who you are or how much you are cherished and adored by your husband and family.

My life story may be unique to my family, but not to my generation. We women born in the 1930s are more alike than different from one another. Many of us have moved from the world bounded by the front yard and inhabited by our families into a world where we are paid for what we do. Some of us are alone and self-supporting now. Others, still married, add important paychecks to the family coffers at a time when additional income is important. Former generations did not do what many of us are doing and we've found few role models among our mothers, much as we love and respect them. Those of us who have made these difficult transitions, who have diffused and shifted the housewife focus to places of work outside our homes, should talk about what we have done, to explain that one can exercise control over what happens in one's life . . . at any age. We can show by a description of our own sometimes uncertain experiences that one can make exciting things happen, even after the terrifying ages of forty or fifty or sixty. Such honest discussion helps others by demonstrating that other women, faced with the same prospects and dilemmas, have been able to deal with them successfully, to make good choices and to move on.

There are things women can do besides live happily ever after with the man of their dreams. This is a valuable lesson because that particular dream can vanish as easily and permanently as the baby once held in your arms.

I remember driving the car someplace one chilly early spring day and having the thought hit me—literally, right in the gut, so I had to take a deep breath and pull over to the side of the road:

"I am forty-one years old."

When had *that* happened? Forty-one? Why wasn't I twenty-six? Or thirty-five? Where had all the years in between gone? I didn't *feel* forty-one. Actually, I felt closer to sixteen. My legs were strong. I could run up a flight of stairs without gasping and panting, I didn't yet have to wear long-sleeved dresses to hide my upper arms; my political and philosophical ideas about Life were still in the process of formation, mostly dependent on the last person I'd spoken to or the latest book I'd read. I still believed what I was told if I admired the teller. I had no answers. Yet until that moment, I had firmly believed people who were forty-one knew all the answers. In addition, and more important, forty-one was *middle-aged.* Where had my thirties gone? I knew my twenties had been spent having babies: My last threadbare maternity dress burst a few weeks after my twenty-seventh birthday, before our youngest, Tom, had been born, leaving me stuffed into unzipped jeans and David's shirts for the last few days before Tom's birth.

What had I done during the next fourteen years? It seemed I ought to be able to remember. Yet I could recall nothing of those days which I knew had carried me, without noticing, inexorably to this age. Forty-one.

For a long time I had been the youngest one, "the kid." Tagging along with my eleven-months older brother when we were little, entering kindergarten with him when he was five and I was four, graduating from high school when I was seventeen and most of the other kids were eighteen.

I was the successful young lawyer's even younger wife with all the little children—eight or ten years younger than the other guests at the dignified dinner parties we went to in the city if I could find a baby-sitter. The few incidents I could remember that happened during my thirties had to do with my husband and my babies: the rollicking evening at the expensive restaurant spent with the two other new partners and their wives when David was made a partner in the law firm; Peter's learning to read before most children his age could talk in sentences; Peggy waking in her crib and singing, sounding like a little bird and thus her brief and appropriate nickname, "Chirpee-Bird"; Carey demanding a ballerina tutu instead of school clothes when she started nursery school (and getting it and wearing it for the first several days, much to the awe and envy of the other children); first-grader Tom running into the house, waving a sheet of yellow lined paper, clutched in his chubby hand: "Look, Mommy! I can make A's! I can make A's!"

All the wonderful, funny, warm memories had to do with other people's achievements. It wasn't that I didn't like the memories, I did, and they filled me with love and made me smile. Yet I wasn't the star of any of them. I was the passive receiver of the good news, the cheerleader, the person on the sidelines feeling proud. My thirties had disappeared and what had I to show for it? What had *I* done?

I took myself in hand and managed to get home from wherever it was I had been driving. I continued thinking about it over the sink scraping carrots that afternoon, and, later that night sipping coffee and looking out the dark kitchen window. I was living the life I had expected to live, of course. All those romantic dreams in high school had been focused on precisely this kind of life.

The astonishing news was that forty-one wasn't old. I had expected it would be, yet it wasn't any different from being thirty-two except there weren't any babies around. The difference was not in the way I felt—I felt the same—it was how the world perceived *me* and how I was programmed to regard women in their forties and older.

I remembered a photograph of my grandmother, my mother's mother, Bawbaw, taken as she held my bundled-up infant brother Clark in the snowy front yard outside my parents' first apartment in Toledo. He was her first grandchild; you could see the pride and reverence on her face as she looked down at him. If I shut my eyes I could hear the sound of her voice. My grandmother: older than anyone, even with her curly dark brown hair (was it dyed?), just as everyone's grandmother is older than anyone, good for baking cookies and worrying about what time you go to bed, without any life outside of responding to the needs of her family, being there to serve them. I figured back, counting on my fingers. How old was Bawbaw in that photograph? Forty-four years old.

She had lived another forty years after that photograph was taken. What had she done all those years? I tried to remember. She had stayed with us for weeks at a time on everlasting visits. (She was not an easy person to get along with.) That had been in Bethesda, Maryland, where my younger brother and sister were born. She also went out to California to be with our uncle and aunt when their babies came, so one of the things she had done during those years was to serve as baby welcomer and expert nurse and housecleaner. Later on, she would come to take care of us when my parents went on trips and, of course, there were the summer visits to her and Grandaddy's big house in Indianapolis. Grandaddy went to the office every day and she stayed home and tended the house and us and took us shopping with her. What had she really been like during those years of stereotypical grandmotherhood?

I suppose I will never have the answer to that question. The picture of a woman without a moment's self-doubt who knew always what was best for herself and for everyone else could not be the answer, although that is how I remember her. The yearning, the aches or confusion she may have felt are lost to my understanding because they were never communicated to me. Somebody's wife, somebody's mother and grandmother was the way she lived out her eighty-four years on earth and I will assume it was a contented life because she worked very hard at transmitting that message to her family.

On the other hand, by the time I reached that momentous day of insight in my car when I suddenly knew I was forty-one, I perceived my life already had become different from the lives led by the women who had preceded me. I hadn't expected such a phenomenon, or prepared for it, but there it was. It occurred to me it was likely I would deviate further as I grew older. The seeds of change had been planted, even though it had not been done on purpose.

The major difference in my life up to then was, at the age of thirty-four, I had returned to college. After being the dumbest kid in my high school class, it was surprising I had done that, especially because nobody in my family had done it before me and people have a way of following in each other's footsteps. I had believed so firmly in my dumbness I can locate precisely in time when I discovered—lo!—I wasn't so dumb after all. At a guitar class I took in 1963, the purpose of which was to get me out of the house for a few hours once a week, it turned out I was, at twenty-eight years of age, the oldest student by fifteen years and the smartest kid in the class. In that dreary church basement I could pick out the chords and understand what the teacher was talking about while the usually intimidating fourteen-year-olds were still grimacing, giggling, punching each other and holding their instruments upside down. (I should add that the class was pre-Dylan; nowadays a three-year-old knows which end of a guitar is up.)

After this heady experience it was only a hop and skip back to college to complete my undergraduate degree (fiercely neglected in the single year spent husband-hunting at DePauw University), and then on to Columbia University for a Master's degree!

I'm not sure now what precipitated this activity, other than the need to prove to myself and to the people around me I was equipped with a perfectly good brain. Whatever the impetus, the result felt wonderful. My husband David was supportive and interested, the kids were proud of me and bragged about my grades. (They almost collapsed when I blithely went off to take my Graduate Record Exam without even knowing the mathematical symbols for "greater than" and "lesser than," old hat to them, products as they were of the incomprehensible New Math.)

I was welcomed to the Center for Continuing Education at Sarah Lawrence College, newly designed and opened for returning students, just like me—long in the tooth and unsure of ourselves, with high achieving husbands who were willing to foot the considerable bill.

The increased intellectual stimulation at an age when my children were becoming increasingly independent helped me live through their various adolescences and to face the fact they were soon to be leaving the nest and that was right and proper. (How terrifying it must have been for Bawbaw when her babies left her. No wonder she seemed always to be hanging around, snooping into our closets. There was nothing else for her to do.)

I was lucky, of course. David was successful and there was money to pay for my tardy education, for a three-mornings-a-week housekeeper to do the stuff which would ordinarily have kept me housebound. (It hadn't always been so. When we were married, in 1956, I was making $80 a week and David $60. That first honeymoon winter we buttoned our overcoats together to make a blanket.)

At forty-one, I had the leisure to reflect on my life,

where it had been and where it was going. I kept thinking about the concept of lifetime marriage, the assumption two people can live together from the time of their early twenties, growing old together and never parting until one of them has died. I had always accepted this ideal as my destiny. Was it going to be possible for me?

I thought not.

David and I were no longer companions. For a long time our marriage had been one of "parallel play." The signals we sent to each other had become mixed and bitter: Instead of feeling grateful, I resented that it was *his* money, *his* effort that gave us the comfortable life we lived, the pervasive presence of which denigrated whatever less tangible contribution I made; he was angry because he felt I did not appreciate the physical and emotional effort providing the money for our life-style cost him. I carped and he withdrew. That had become the story of our marriage.

Most of us have grown up to think the success of a marriage is measured by its longevity; possibly there are other determinants. The goal of a lifetime marriage is idealized by most people my age, no matter what the state of their own marriages. I wonder if there are other kinds of marriages, successful in their own ways, which are not "lifetime." I am reminded of the stranger who asks the front-porch-sitting New Englander, "Have you lived here all your life?" "Not yet," replies the old-timer. You don't know if you're in a lifetime marriage until one of you has died.

Our marriage ended when I was forty-three. Although it ended, ours was not a "bad" marriage. The finished marriage produced no villains. We had grown in different directions, but we did not hate each other, in fact, spent many happy times together and continue to be fond of one another. David was the right person for me to marry in 1956. I have no regrets, except that low-level ache that always accompanies the passage of time, the ache that comes with the knowledge that something precious has vanished, and one can do nothing about it.

Two years before we divorced I knew it was imperative I get a job. College was ended, the children were well on

their way to adulthood. I come from a long line of long-
lived people. I figured that, unless I was hit by a Greyhound
bus, it was likely I would live to the age of eighty-five or
even older. I drew a line on a piece of paper and marked it
off like this:

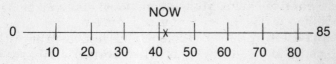

I studied the drawing for a long time. There was as
much life ahead of me on the graph as there was behind me.

I wanted to occupy the years in the second half of my
lifeline as fully and with as much commitment and enjoy-
ment as I had the first half. There was no road map for this
second half as there had been for the first. I would have to
find my own landmarks, invent my future in ways that had
never before occurred to me—or my mother, or my
grandmother. I realized I would have to observe and learn
about what other women had done and were doing.
Evidently there were a lot of hidden things about woman-
hood not included with the script I'd been studying.

At first, and for a long time, I didn't think what other
women had done and were doing was pertinent to me. I did
not consider myself a "feminist" in the early seventies (by
the time I got around to reading *The Feminine Mystique*,
published in 1963, it was 1978). I thought the difficulties I
faced were mine alone. In my family it was a sin to be
boring so I avoided the opportunity to discuss my personal
uneasiness even with my friends. I assumed they wouldn't
understand anyway (their houses were always much
neater than mine). For a long time I struggled with the
secret belief that I was that rare and shameful specimen, a
failed housewife. I didn't know anybody else who felt that
way. How could I? All of us would have died before
admitting it.

My friends were all married mothers, as I was. Stories
about bra-burning and ERA marches made us click our
tongues with disapproval. Why make people look at you
and notice how inappropriately you are behaving? Why
didn't these unsound women go home and scrub out their

undoubtedly dirty toilets? None of us in Pleasantville were in the forefront of the Women's Movement and, indeed, were suspicious of those who were.

Later, it took me a while before I was able to look people in the eye when my marriage ended. I felt isolated and different from them. My self-consciousness about being an unorthodox middle-aged ex-married person prevented me from expecting fair treatment and respect from other people in the same way as when formerly I had been secretly mortified about being the world's worst house-wife, or, before that, the klutziest co-ed, or, even earlier, the most unpopular girl in school or the one who couldn't climb the ropes in gym class. Feelings of failure isolate you: You're supposed to be a winner, not a loser. The way to be a winner-housewife was to have a kitchen floor people could see their faces in.

Had I understood and empathized with other women who were coming to grips with the unfairly limiting treatment we had grown up with and *never even noticed*, I might have avoided the terrible burden of role-failure, or at least have had somebody else to talk with about it. But mine is the story of a conventional person, an armchair radical who has been reluctant always to leave the cozy living room to say brave things or to risk in any way that safe and comfortable life. The abstract battle against injustice and the seductive life in the house on the hill have both attracted me since I was a romantic little girl longing to be Napoleon (not Josephine) and at the same time drawing pictures of Prince Charming carrying off the princess (me) on his white horse.

All this serves to demonstrate that when I started looking for a career outside my home, it did not occur to me that the conventions of the culture I was part of served to put me at a disadvantage. I believed anyhow that "nice people" don't speak of it if they notice someone behaving unfairly to them. While organizing with other women to demand equal treatment was an admirable act of out-spoken women in history, I believed in the United States of America in the 1970s that problem had gone away and no longer needed to be addressed. (We had the vote, didn't we?) Clearly, Black people and poor people had legitimate gripes. My inclination was to stand up for these obviously just causes and put the murky and nameless problem of middle-class women on a distant back burner.

In 1975, when I tackled the job market, I was still married and still living in Pleasantville, although the days there were numbered. I realized the contribution I, an ex-housewife, could make was not what the corporate world had been holding its breath to receive. It was clear to me—and to all my expert advisors, from the butcher at the Pleasantville Super Market, to Patty T., my next door neighbor, who had taught math to junior high school children taller than herself while her husband was getting his M.B.A. at the University of Chicago, then retired to have *her* four children, to Doris H., whose husband had run off with the minister's secretary and who, with a job at a chic local boutique, made $120 a week and looked, with her aristocratically high hollow cheeks and greenish complexion, like she was starving to death—that no one would hire me because I was "just a housewife."

My Puritan Ethic belief was you must earn rewards and be punished for failure; if you're not having a good time, that is *good for you.* Making yourself do something you hate because it is your duty is *admirable.* After nineteen years, I had not yet learned to be the kind of good housewife we all revere on television. No one was going to reward me with a paid job. I didn't deserve it.

The world of work was a magic place where people spoke a language I did not understand, did things I was not able to do, earned money for accomplishing totally alien and mysterious tasks about which I knew nothing. I knew nothing about The Office except that David (like my father and grandfather before him) went there every morning and returned every night and every couple of weeks brought home a bag of money from it.

It terrified me to enter that world. I believed myself to be inept, incompetent and useless in such a place, habituated by Important Men with Briefcases. No wonder women like me were paid low wages, I thought. What a miracle to be paid at all!

I began to read the want ads and Employment Opportunities columns. I saw there were no jobs available which fit my particular qualifications (or lack of them). Want ad pages tended to organize themselves by jobs that had names: bookkeeper, accountant, actuary, pharmacist, engineer, chemist, etc. Since I wasn't any of these things, about 90 percent of the help wanted ads were of no value to me. More general "college graduate" categories invariably included entry level jobs, mostly with publishers. This was a field in which I was interested, but I knew I would be competing with fresh young Ivy Leaguers for the sought-after $135-a-week starting salaries. In my forties, I had been a "go-fer" (go-fer coffee, go-fer the paper, go-fer a box of pencils for the boss-husband-child) for so long I knew I wouldn't be able to manage it at The Office, too. I wanted more than a change of scenery in the job I was going to find. Much as I yearned for my very own paycheck, I didn't want more low-profile, servant-mode tasks. Although publishing was an area I was attracted to, I grasped I must locate an unconventional, unusual place which would afford me a leg up and over the other, younger beginners by recognizing my gifts and ability (even if I couldn't) and setting me to work at a job I could get my long teeth into. The big, well-established publishers of books were all enticingly headquartered in New York City, only a short train ride from where I lived, but I knew they would not consider an aged housewife, even if I didn't tell them my immediate goal was to be an editor at *The New Yorker*. Although I continued to scrutinize the jobs listed under "publishing" and "college graduates" I knew I would probably not find Nirvana there.

Other areas I studied in the paper had to do with jobs titled "administrative assistant" and secretaries. I knew how to type; I enjoyed typing. It is a mindless task, one which affords the rare and delightful opportunity to daydream. When you're done, you have a nice neat important-looking finished product. Typing is like vacuuming or doing the dishes and needs approximately the same brain candlepower. However, I decided any job in which the primary task was typing would be unacceptable to me because I wanted to be able to think and to superimpose my own special style and interests on whatever job I was doing.

Many years before, I had been a secretary. After my single year of college, when I decided to come to New York and become an actress (a short-lived goal since, once I got to New York, I never had the nerve to make rounds or *even to find out how one made rounds*), my father okayed the plan but stipulated I would first have to learn shorthand and typing. His reason, and it was not the slightest bit facetious, serving yet again to demonstrate the status of women in the American culture of the 1950s, was the following: There are only two job possibilities for unmarried, unemployed women (actresses are always unemployed): being a secretary or being a prostitute. Ergo, I was to learn shorthand and typing.

Still living at home, I attended business college for three months, where I learned to type. Mastering the vagaries of Gregg shorthand proved more elusive. After a while, when I could no longer tolerate my commercial course in those stuffy rooms above the drugstore, I managed to land a secretarial job at a small factory in East Toledo where I labored for several months. When I left for New York City, I was an excellent typist.

Twenty-two years later I keenly remembered the struggles I'd had with the shorthand; I contemplated my bad spelling which had never improved and my difficulty in accepting the role of the unsung hero. I decided I didn't want to be a secretary again. Because of this decision, my options, at least insofar as the want ads were concerned, were definitely limited. I started reading other kinds of ads, ads that talked about career counseling, resumé-writing, self-selling programs. Most of these ads seemed to be geared to people already employed, but at least two of them might have been addressed to my special inexperience. One outfit was called "Midlife" ("Want to Reassess your MIDLIFE Goals?") and the other "New Careers." I telephoned them both and when a representative of New Careers returned my call first, I picked them.

I reserved a place in the New Careers workshop, three days in a small two-story house with a carefully tended front lawn next door to a funeral parlor in Montclair, New Jersey. A couple of weeks in advance of the workshop I took a long aptitude test, the results of which indicated I was suited to be a sales person, a social worker or editor of a small-town newspaper, all of which fitted into the nice fantasies I had always nurtured (and perhaps directed my test answers toward?). Less inspirational information had to do with my feelings about homely pursuits like baking apples, sewing, and wallpapering the bathroom, which scored so low they didn't even get numbers affixed after them on the assessment sheet—surprise, surprise.

The workshop was geared to people who wanted to "change career direction" in the middle of their lives. Sessions were designed to ferret out the occupational skills developed by many years of experience. It was *skills* (development skills, organizational or motivational and administrative skills), not job titles the teachers were interested in. It was an interesting approach. I was surprised at the resistance the idea met with among the men. As it happened, perhaps sixteen of the twenty-five people in attendance were men. They resisted the unconventional skills-identification technique, probably because they had important sounding titles which demonstrated they were significant persons, not to be trifled with—even if they didn't want to do any more of whatever it was their titles said they did.

Each man seemed to have unique reasons for wanting to change his career, none having to do with self-doubt or lack of competence. They seemed quite comfortable with the presumption that with proper instruction they could change careers. They were here, sensibly, to learn how to accomplish this, even though they ended up behaving as if the instructors' heads were full of cheese and most of them went home announcing they might as well have thrown their money out the window for all the help the workshop lessons would give them. They were a stubborn lot. They argued and disagreed with the teachers without apprehension (unlike the women). Most of them were so sure of themselves I figured they would all leave and do pretty much what they had planned to do anyhow.

I've often wondered why they rejected the approach so emphatically. As I remember it, the workshop lessons were based on the premise that a job—any job—ultimately takes on the profile of the person holding it. Therefore, any campaign to find another job must reflect the strengths (skills) already developed by the job seeker in jobs held prior to that person's current search (even a voluntary career like a housewife). Skills are not job titles, they are better and more useful because skills are transferrable from industry to industry, department to department, in a school system or at Exxon Corporation, in sales jobs or finance jobs or research jobs. Titles are self-limiting. They don't hold within them the story of what you do. If you want to change your career, your potential employer must understand what you're good at. The ways you solved problems at your last jobs are part of your personal style and can be defined specifically as "skills." It is common sense to figure out your skills and to write your resumé emphasizing these strong points. Potential employers must be able to determine how you will fit within their organizations, and scrutiny of your experience and the skills you have developed is a major part of how they can best make this determination.

This common-sense approach, which is fairly widely accepted now, was too unconventional in 1975, at least in Montclair, New Jersey.

Unlike the cocky, sure-of-themselves men, the women at the workshop were shaking in their boots. Like me, they were all housewives: They didn't believe anybody could show them how they were skilled because it was clear to them they were not. They all sounded alike: "I'm just a housewife. I can't do anything but my children are all grown up now (or my husband has run off and left me or had a stroke or I'm a widow), and I have to find some kind of a job." They never referred to it as a "career," but always a "job," somehow sounding second class and inferior in their aspirations, wanting only to secure a steady paycheck which would pay the monthly grocery bill or keep them in gas and curlers. Personal satisfaction wasn't part of the equation. Because they believed only a miracle could help them they were heartbreakingly obedient and polite, lacking the pep that produces enthusiasm. They were willing to try anything suggested, no matter how outlandish, because they had no ability to evaluate career possibilities or to figure out the choices open to them, if any. They were so used to playing the role of housewife, they were so used to degrading themselves in that role, they could not envision themselves doing anything else. We worked hard during the three days to please the instructors, to do exactly as we were told.

I tried to put myself in the position of an employer. I wouldn't want to hire a whiner either, but there was more to it than that. These women operated under a gigantic handicap of low self-esteem which was manifest in constant apologizing and deference. One woman had managed her physician husband's office for years. Her daily routine included all the record keeping, dealing with drug "detail" men and with patients, the necessary purchasing and billing, and simultaneous raising of their three children and supervision of a household that also included several exuberant animals. Yet she suffered from a devastating lack of confidence, making her end every sentence with a question mark.

When I looked at this beautifully dressed, elegant-looking woman, I knew she was precisely the competent kind of person who had always made me feel inferior and overweight. Here she was, being honest, allowing her fright to show, vulnerable, uncertain. She was more like me than I'd imagined. She, too, felt as if she didn't measure up. It was a revelation.

Each of us could afford to spend $900 on a three-day workshop but I wondered how many of us could change our attitudes about ourselves in such a short period of time. It seemed unlikely.

In addition, I couldn't help thinking about the other women out there who couldn't afford to take the station wagon into Montclair for a three-day think-about-yourself session, as we had done. I suppose this was the first creaking, reluctant "raising of consciousness" I experienced. I went off to begin my job campaign and didn't think much more about The Women. It turned out, however, that the subject would become a major preoccupation in my life.

CHAPTER TWO

My Job Campaign,
My Job and My Business

AT THE NEW CAREERS WORKSHOP MY NEW FRIENDS and I had learned 80 percent of all "new hires" come about because of personal contacts—friends, relatives, friends of friends and relatives. That made sense, yet many of us were reluctant to approach people we knew, particularly if they were successful executive types. As housewives, we felt outside the clan, without measurable value in a world where value is determined by price. There was no price tag affixed to our daily routine. Looking for paid work outside our homes, we were pears in a world of oranges. Even when we talked to old friends, if they had worked for pay all their adult lives, the distance across the desk between us became a time warp, a million years of difference.

One of my big fears was I didn't know how to talk about myself and what I did in the same way the people at the office talked about themselves and their jobs. I was afraid my ignorance would be a flag, despite the careful interviewing script our workshop leaders had worked out for us. This ignorance of office jargon made me feel uncomfortable, even more of an outsider.

In the spring of 1975, in order to combat the real enemy—not inexperience, but this feeling of being on the outside looking in—I tried to remember I was armed with a job-market plan of action for which I had paid $900, a constant reminder of the plan's real-world value. It had been designed, not by me, but by experts, people who knew what they were talking about, business people who designed job campaigns *for a living*. They and I had worked up a brand-new impressive-sounding resumé that talked about my "skills" (not shorthand and typing) and described cogently the experience I had gained as a worker and candidate in local politics, a volunteer and part-time counselor in the local drug rehabilitation center, as a freelance (unpaid) movie reviewer for a local newspaper. (I didn't include in my resumé the time I had raved about a quickly vanished film called *The Fortune* and was later assailed on the street by a disgruntled stranger who said she would never believe anything I wrote again.) My resumé was one page long, its printed and expensive-looking format adding legitimacy to my persona. I began to feel optimistic.

My next step was to buy a supply of index cards and a box to keep them in. Each card was for the name of a different person I knew. I spent an afternoon looking up their telephone numbers and addresses and carefully transcribing them on the cards. I left plenty of room under each name for a report on the meeting I would have with that particular person. I would initiate each meeting myself. I would talk about my skills and demonstrate through my businesslike demeanor I was "good material." I would not flutter and flicker and fizzle as if I were on a blind date. I would lead the conversation and make sure the points I wanted to talk about were covered. We had "role played" at the workshop—one of the teachers sitting with one of the students in front of everybody else, leading them through a pretend conversation/interview. It worked like a charm at the workshop. I believed with my usual innocent and unsubstantiated conceit I had been one of the best role-players, indeed, the teacher's pet. I was eager to apply the new interviewing skill in the real world.

The job market I was going after was hidden. It had

nothing to do with ads in the paper and articles about the "job climate" in business publications. The workshop leaders had told us most management job openings are *not* advertised; often people leave their jobs and new people are hired to replace them without the intervention of an employment agency or an ad. This was particularly true, according to New Careers, in lower- and middle-executive, or "decision-making" positions, which were the kind of positions I wanted and they had helped me to come to believe I was qualified for. Friends were always talking to each other about personnel needs. "Call Charlie." This was why it was important to talk to as many people as you knew because the names of the people to whom you had already spoken served as entrée to the next and all successive "generations." The job was there, somewhere, in that vast interconnecting fabric of personal contacts.

Working from the index cards, I began to call up people I knew, telling them I was embarked on a job search, making appointments with them to discuss my "exploration of the job market." I wasn't to ask anyone point-blank for a job— that was threatening and definitely *verboten.* These initial discussions with my friends were to circumvent the failures and mishaps that occurred when conventional job-search methods, like answering want ads, were used. I was to go to my friends, present myself as a qualified and intelligent candidate for employment (not necessarily in my friend's firm), obtain names of their friends for my next wave of telephone calls. The first visit was to set off a chain reaction of contacts and sooner or later one of the members of one of these generations of people would offer me a pleasing and appropriate job.

That's the way the old-boy process had always operated and that was the way it was going to operate for this new personnel resource, returning housewife me.

Our mottos at the workshop were Never Accept the First Offer and Don't Take a Job You Don't Want.

Of course I was terrified. I tried to remember my acting teacher's admonition "run toward your fear," and my own Dirty Diaper Axiom: When you see your child running around in a dirty diaper, change it *immediately.* If you ignore it, it will *get worse.* So, I bit the bullet, picked up the telephone and started dialing people on my list who included one of David's well-connected law partners, head of my town's political party, wife of one of David's clients who worked for a private foundation, the advertising executive husband of one of the children's former teachers, etc.

People were gratifyingly helpful, as the workshop had predicted they would be. David's law partner obligingly went through his Rolodex and came up with ten or fifteen names of his friends who were engaged in various unusual and interesting pursuits. One of them invited me to spend an entire afternoon with her at a social agency which did research for studies on various current issues ranging from the problems of ghetto schools to teen-age mothers to old people and nursing homes. Another friend of a friend managed a firm which represented musicians, kind of a rock band Sol Hurok. He recommended I visit with a friend of his in the textbook department of a major publisher. Before I was able to make that appointment (I was seeing three or four people a week and my list of others still to see was actually growing faster than my ability or desire to make appointments with them), I visited somebody who was president of a small executive recruiting firm (who knew what executive recruiting was?). During our pleasant, low-key conversation, he glanced at my resumé and said, "Tell me about your Master's Degree in American History." I replied—and I had not planned this exchange, I will never know why I said it, why it came so easily, but these things happen and I am a believer in luck—"That doesn't mean I'm an expert in American History, it means I'm an expert in research."

I was unaware he and his partner had decided that morning to hire a research manager. In fact, when I realized the interview had changed character and become an interview for a *specific job* instead of the present-my-skills-ask-for-referrals interview, which was all I had prepared for, everything went blank. I was not prepared for a specific job interview, even though that was the ostensible purpose of all of my preparation, the card file and the telephoning and the identification and innumeration of my impressive sounding skills, the meetings with perfect strangers. That was the fly in the ointment of the workshop lessons. I had no idea how to proceed, how to behave once I was zeroing in on a real job.

I had planned a leisurely unpressured exploration of the job market which would last three to six months, a process wherein I would meet and talk with many interesting people before I would gradually modify my interview presentation and close in on the kill. Here it was happening in this office with the rosewood paneling and the purple carpeting scarcely a month after the workshop! I was abysmally unprepared for questions having to do with my qualifications for a specific job and I felt myself turning to seaweed.

"Tell me about yourself," said stone-jawed Mel, in that age-old open-ended way interviewers have, and I, thinking myself ready for him, responded I was "intelligent and creative." My glibness vanished when he followed (quite logically) with: "Give me an example of your creativity." I could think of nothing, no example of anything creative I had ever done, I felt slow-witted, boring, without imagination, a lump of unrisen bread dough.

At this moment I cannot remember what answer I finally invented; I know its inadequacy must have embarrassed Mel as much as it did me because he never mentioned it again, to my great relief and gratitude.

My inability to deal with discussion in which the direct purpose was a job offer, and not a referral, stemmed from my basic inability to think of myself, despite all the encouragement and all the plans formulated at the workshop, as a valuable personnel resource. I hadn't really come such a long way from the kitchen. I was too ready to jump in anywhere, to do anything, to please and obey my commander-in-chief. I was still unwilling to put job satisfaction high on my list of priorities. Whether or not he wanted *me* instantly took precedence over all other considerations.

At the workshop, far away from the seductive environment of this office, this desk—which might, please God, someday be mine—we had decided definitely not to take the first offer that came along, no matter how tempting it was. Despite these best laid plans, I was ready to accept the job, whatever it was, as soon as it was offered, even if it required nothing more mind-stretching than typing lists of invoice numbers day after day.

I hung in there, though, clamped my mouth shut and said nothing to improve my chances . . . or ruin them.

A couple of weeks later, after the two partners had each met separately with me and then conferred with each other, Howard offered me the job. I had to grip the arms of the chair in order to refrain from throwing myself across his tasseled shoes. Of course I accepted.

No matter my beginning salary was $11,000 per year ($212 per week) and David's new 22-year-old secretary made $15,000. She was highly trained, after all, and I was only a housewife.

No matter I had planned to pursue my job search in an orderly, mature, well-organized manner, coldly assessing each possibility, finding out everything I could about whatever the business was, how it fit into the profit-making world in general, what specific duties I would handle, what goals and expectations my potential employer had for me and how those plans dovetailed with my own plan for growth and fulfillment. I had been determined not to allow my head to be turned by the mere offer of steady work and here I was, my head not just turning, but spinning.

So much for objectivity, for a common-sense approach to my own job campaign. I started the job three weeks later.

Ordinarily, the first priority, when you are a working mother, is to see that everybody at home is fed and otherwise cared for. For some reason, even with both parents working, the PTA membership, the open houses and ballet lessons, the Brownie meetings and school plays and bake sales, the meal preparation, laundry, vacuum cleaning and all other assorted homefront tasks are still relegated to The Mom. Of course it's unfair, but that's how it is—at least so far as women in my generation are concerned. And as long as there exists such "woman's work," every working woman will have two jobs. It comes down to what my brilliant blue-eyed, blond political science professor told me once, stuffing papers into her briefcase as we both hurried home in order to be in time to fix our respective family's suppers: "Every working woman needs a wife."

When I returned to paid work, I lived in Pleasantville, New York, a pretty suburban village in Westchester County, an hour's train ride from New York City. My children ranged in age from fourteen-year-old Tom, in the eighth grade in the Pleasantville Middle School, to Peter, eighteen, away from home and a freshman at Oberlin College in Ohio.

When I began my daily commute, everybody in the family had to adjust to the new situation. David had to get used to my lengthy presence in the bathroom when he had, heretofore, always had it to himself in the mornings. The children's eyes widened with amazement when I hurried into the kitchen at 7:15 A.M. in makeup and *high heeled shoes.*

It was all a startling change, but we managed. Since no one had been used to pheasant under glass for dinner, it was not missed. People pitched in. Our house was even less orderly than before and it lurched along for a while, but the new arrangement worked because we all wanted it to work.

I had good luck in my job, too, for reasons unclear to me when I accepted the offer. An advantage occurred right off the bat when my new boss gave me my first week off with pay. There was trouble in the office, an unhappy partner had just exploded out of the small firm and there was great upheaval and concern. Howard told me he would not have sufficient opportunity those first few days to teach me the ropes, so we would wait until there was enough and more relaxed time. I was asked to stay home for a week at full pay. ("Gee, I really like my job," I effused.) In fact, the first Monday I did report I found an armed guard seated at the door.

That appeared to be the last of the dramatic incidents, though, and I rolled up the sleeves of my new camel's hair blazer and addressed learning what I was supposed to do. Landing my first job in this particular function (research) in this particular area (executive recruiting) was propitious. It was an ideal spot for an outsider to learn about the business world. In many ways the orientation and training for my job resembled a course at business school: I had to learn and use the lingo, figure out how companies were organized, learn enough about what I was looking for so I could ask intelligent questions. My job was *to find out* and I had to invent ways to do so. I was enthusiastic, intrepid. *I was being paid.*

Executive recruiters are hired by companies to provide qualified candidates for their clients' specific job openings. They do not work for the people who want to be placed, but, instead, for the companies that have jobs to fill. The kinds of people they place is controlled by the needs of their clients. If a terrific financial analyst walks in the recruiter's door in need of a job, the recruiter really can't help him unless one of his clients needs a financial analyst. He may make a few telephone calls (the old-boys again), but the "walk-in" is probably out of luck, no matter how expert he is at what he does.

Basically, as research manager in such a firm, I had to locate people who were doing the kind of work that fit the client's description of the job opening. Often I had to establish that the potential candidates I unearthed had outstanding reputations or some special expertise before the recruiter met with them. After receiving the names of such people from me, the recruiter would interview and evalute their possible "fit." Then he would either present the likeliest of the lot to his client, or write them off and ask me for more. Most recruiters like to present the client with three or four potential candidates for each opening, so when the research is done in the beginning, approximately fifteen or twenty people's names must be provided for him to sift through. In order to collect this data and to insure its appropriateness, I had to make sure when I was looking for it I understood precisely what was called for in the job description. This necessitated a thorough briefing with the recruiter (I wasn't allowed to talk to the client), and then telephone calls to experts in various pertaining fields, who, as a rule, were helpful when I contacted them and asked them questions. Since all of these calls were "cold"—I had no idea what the person I was talking to looked like or what would please or irritate him—it was necessary for me to develop a winning telephone manner. Sometimes I was a dumb, helpless kid who would be fired if she didn't get the right kind of information (Judy Holliday), or, on other occasions, when it seemed more appropriate, I would be smart, tough and impatient (Glenda Jackson). Since both personalities exist simultaneously in my semi-schizo-phrenic character, this wasn't as hard to manage as it might sound.

As part of my job I spoke on the telephone to professors and heads of departments at places like Yale, MIT, Harvard, the Universities of Chicago or Wisconsin, experts in the federal government at the Bureau of Standards and in the Public Health Service, as well as captains and generals in industry. I was able to talk to these important people, people I didn't even know, because I was old enough to understand people will usually answer questions if they are good questions, even if they are asked by strangers. That was a valuable insight and I think I had to be over thirty-five to comprehend its truth.

I might ask a professor of mechanical engineering at Georgia Tech, for example, to describe an imaginary work profile of an outstanding student who had gone into work which involved the development of ultrasound or other "imaging" equipment. I might ask him for recommendations of people he felt filled the bill for the position when I described it to him. Sometimes I called editors of trade publications to find out who they knew to be outstanding people in particular fields. I was a member (briefly) of the Society for Heat, Ventilating and Air Conditioning in order to obtain a directory of its members but never attended a meeting so never learned the Society song or handshake. I spoke to executives at companies involved in the details of meat processing, cardboard box manufacturing, toxicology research and silvaculture. I could not start telephoning until I knew enough to ask good solid basic questions, and I constructed the foundations for this knowledge myself by clipping and reading business publications on file in the office. Sometimes I would haunt the Readers' Guide at the public library and undergo frustrating hours of groping through the mysteries of the inconstant microfilm machines, most of which chronically malfunctioned. With every article I read and every phone call I made, my knowledge expanded. I think there are few other jobs I could have started out in that would have trained me so well. I hit the ground running.

As I became accustomed to the business world, I learned it was not at all a place of mystery but a place, of course, like the world in which I had always lived. People everywhere had the same kinds of problems. In Pleasantville one of my neighbors had been arrested by the embarrassed local police chief for drunken driving at nine-thirty one Tuesday morning after attempting to park the family station wagon within the brand-new plate-glass front doors of Barclay's Hardware. At work, a secretary got fired after habitually reeling around the office in a bleary haze, smelling like bourbon-soaked breath fresheners. The crisis came one afternoon when she sat for an hour or so, silently and with some bafflement, gazing at her typewriter and then crouched behind the door and sprang out shouting "Boo!" as her harried boss walked in with a client. Clients, and how one behaves in front of them, are hallowed and revered beyond the first meeting of the in-laws, so that was the end of her.

It took me about eight months to achieve a thorough understanding of the research process as it applied to business research and to be confidant I had become an expert in it. Then, being ambitious and upwardly mobile, I started figuring out what my next step should be. No matter how necessary their work in the overall scheme or how highly competent they are, in a recruiting firm, researchers are almost always pigeonholed as "clerical" employees. I grasped the real action lay with recruiting itself. Not only were the recruiters able to learn about businesses as I was learning about businesses, but they had the fun of interviewing candidates and dealing closely with clients. Most important, because their jobs were closer to the firm's main artery—income and profit making—their potential for making big money was much greater than mine in both the short and the long range. Recruiters work on a percentage of the fee basis (they usually get a third of the company's fee on the jobs on which they work), rather than a straight salary. For example, if the firm's total fee on a particular job amounts to $15,000, the recruiter who handles the assignment will be paid a third of that fee, or

$5,000. I saw this was a much more lucrative arrangement than my straight salary. (Some sage once pointed out that nobody ever got rich on salary.) I thought I would enjoy making a lot of money at least as much as I did learning about the business world, especially if the two went hand in hand. After more than a year and three raises, I was still making an annual salary of less than $14,000, even though I knew I was doing a good job and was valuable to the firm. I made less than $14,000, even including the profit sharing plan (a mysterious and unpredictable sum—a couple of hundred dollars—added to my "account" at the end of each year, mine when I left the company), and my bonus. The bonus, hard cash, came regularly at the end of the firm's fiscal year and was determined without a formula by the two partners. Although they figured it in as part of my annual compensation and included it as if it were an integral part of my salary when they discussed my progress with me at my year's end review, the bonus could be anything (I had no control over it) and was far from automatic. It was a large part of my income and averaged between $1,500 and $3,000. The bonus would be withheld from my final paycheck if I left the company before the end of its fiscal year, although that fact was never discussed. When I left the April 15th before the fiscal year's end, August 31, I received no part of my bonus.

When Howard talked with me about my "compensation package" and included the bonus as part of that figure, we both knew he was talking about an incentive to insure my hard work. It was never an inherent part of my salary, it was a unilaterally determined reward and it was his leverage.

Once, early on, when I volunteered to stay after work one night to get some urgent project done, Howard responded in a decidedly Dickensian tone, "there is no such thing as 'after work.'" All well and good for him, was my cowardly unspoken response, since he owned the company and took home an annual $100,000 or so, but I was making $12,000 a year at the time, and it was difficult for me to understand why my commitment and devotion to the firm should have been as great as his.

I was keeping my eyes open and I was learning. Those

things I was learning were not restricted to business and organizational theory. There were hard facts to learn and apply involving payroll and bonus plans and responsibility and authority and a "what's in it for me?" aspect never before part of my mind-set. I was learning how to be a businesswoman.

When I understood the game and the players, I knew I wanted to get off salary and onto a percentage deal. Howard agreed with me and gave me reason to believe I was being groomed for "consultant" status.

Progress along these lines was slower than I thought it ought to be. After two and a half years I was interviewing potential candidates, making evaluations and writing "profiles" (work experience biographies intended for the client, much more detailed than resumés, usually three or four, or more, pages in length). In fact, I was doing pretty much of everything except meeting with clients and negotiating the final arrangements between them and the candidate— difficult to do since I was not allowed to deal with the clients. I was still on salary ($15,000) and was promoted to something called a "consulting associate," but Howard and Mel were evidently not as sanguine about my capacity for speedy forward progress as I was.

Earlier, while I was still married, I had decided to remain patient because I was starting out on what I hoped would be a long and prosperous career, and learning while I earned. I believed I would be rewarded for my hard work and perseverance. (Note the passive nature of my objective. I *would be rewarded.* I still believed I would be taken care of if I ate all my spinach and was a good little girl.) But the golden ring seemed to get farther away the more I learned and the harder I worked.

When I because a Consulting Associate, beautiful business cards were printed for me and I was moved into a posh new office which I decorated in a deep teal green, but my progress was primarily cosmetic.

As I became more confident at my job, David and I were becoming more certain that it was the time to end our marriage. For me, the courage to face the reality came in direct proportion to my increasing feelings of competence at work. I do not think I could have faced life alone with all the struggles and the changes I knew would come, coupled with new and awful solitude, without the sense of self-esteem which came about because of my new-found ability to perform well as a paid worker in a world of paid workers. It is difficult to manage radical change in your personal life if you are paralyzed with fear you won't be able to pull it off and have no evidence anywhere in your workaday life that change is something you can handle. By returning to paid work I had demonstrated to myself I could cope with important change. When it turned out I was good at what I did and not a bumbling and ineffective bathrobed creature from the car pool, when I saw I was able to earn the respect of my superiors and my peers, a feeling quite special and unfamiliar, then I thought I would be able to handle whatever came next. I was no longer the trusting little girl awaiting somebody's permission to get on with my life. I felt almost able to take care of myself. So David left amicably and started his new life and I got on with mine.

My strengthening attitude altered my perceptions of my role at work. From one angle, I appreciated Howard and Mel's concern about me. I liked them and was grateful they had given me, somebody unknown and inexperienced, a chance. Yet the setup in their company limited me, now that I wanted to go further, because it was arranged on a patriarchal mode. The assumption was not only did Howard and Mel know best how fast I should develop and what I should be doing, but also how I should dress and talk and behave. By being docile and obedient I was giving them the same power over my life I had given my father and my husband. It was difficult to learn the difference between legitimate gripes and proper businesslike behavior, though. Of course the principals in a business know what direction their company is going and what they want their employees to do while at work, but there is room for differing management styles in order to achieve these goals; the differences between professional and personal advice is a fairly distinct one when the office is run on a professional and not a patriarchal basis. Some bosses would never think they had the right to tell a grown-up employee (man or woman) they "ought to do something" with their hair, although Howard told me that during one of our work sessions. Was I being oversensitive or was that an inappropriate factor to impose on one's professional evaluation and development? Was he telling me that out of kindness, or was there a deeper message, something along the lines of my not being allowed out of the back office until I "did something" with my hair? I wasn't taking any chances. I began to spend money at the beauty parlor.

On the other hand, there are distinct advantages to playing the role of child in a patriarchal hierarchy. Often your daddy will put you under his wing and take you places you would otherwise be unable to go.

Our firm belonged to the elitist executive recruiting trade association, and once Howard invited me to accompany him to one of the elegant dinner meetings. I was grateful and vowed to myself I would behave decorously and intelligently. This proved more difficult than it might appear.

First of all, many of the old executive recruiting firms were dominated by WASP Ivy League men. Reality is that at least half of the top-flight business school graduates since the Second World War represent people of Italian, Jewish, Irish, Slavic and other persuasions, so executive recruiters have had to widen their ranks to reflect this change, just as has American business in general. The fact their monthly meetings are held in New York City's exclusive University Club, which has never accepted women as members, indicates a blind spot the executive recruiting society has not yet addressed. This unspoken bias is, of course, made clear by the selection of the University Club for the regular meetings. Being discreet and shunning flamboyant unpleasantness, they need to make no other statement.

It became clear to me as soon as I walked in I was a mutation of some exotic variety, there being only five other women present. Howard had brought his female assistant, Eleanor, and I recognized another woman who was secretary to the Society's Executive Director. I didn't know who the other three women guests were. There were approximately sixty-five men in attendence. Howard introduced me to a few people during the cocktail hour, then left me alone, which was fine with me and indicated his trust.

At dinner I picked a table peopled with some recruiters I didn't know. The man on my right, a representative of a search firm whose first and second tiers of management were reputed to be populated exclusively with Yale men, took one flickering glance at me and did not speak a word other than "pass the salt" to me during the meal. I was irritated by the snub but reflected since my daughter Peggy was attending Yale at that very moment, even his short-sighted eyes would have to focus on a female executive recruiter sooner or later. I talked to the people on my left and across from me. I was pleased I did nothing which might have embarrassed Howard and after the slide presentation and discussion following dinner, I went over to thank him for bringing me and made ready to go.

Complications ensued.

The huge paneled banquet room was in the nether regions of the club's first floor and I wasn't sure how to get to the cloakroom to retrieve my coat. I spotted two men by the door who seemed about to leave, and said to them, "Would you mind escorting me to the place we checked our coats?" My mistake was to add irreverently, "I'm afraid I will step on some hallowed floorboard and be struck by lightning."

One of the men stopped smiling and drew himself up to his full height of five foot, six inches. "I am on the Board of Governors of the University Club and as long as I am, I will never vote to accept women as members," he said, somewhat gratuitously, I felt. I checked the immediate flush of temper which burned my cheeks and remembered that my boss had brought me and expected me to behave with dignity. I responded in as mild a tone as I could muster, "Yes, I'm aware of the University Club's policy about not allowing women as members. That's why I asked you to take me to the cloakroom. I didn't want to wander around and, perhaps, blunder into someplace where I'm not allowed. I've never been here before."

He continued to glare at me; his companion looked embarrassed, I was glad to note, and then, curiously, he repeated his statement in exactly the same words and tone of voice, as if the message had been prerecorded:

"I am on the Board of Governors of the University Club and as long as I am, I will never vote to accept women as members."

I saw red. Once was quite enough. I remembered my friend Margie's remark that a lady is never unintentionally rude and I pulled myself up to my full height so I was clearly looking down at him. I said in my most steely toned, Toledo-elitist voice, "Yes, I know of your policy, *sir*. I have read your by-laws (I had, in the days of sweet ignorance when I thought it would be nice to join a club where I could take other business people for lunch) and am familiar with the language. Nowhere does it say the University Club is a social club for men only. The by-laws clearly state its membership is restricted to graduates of accredited colleges and universities. Since I have earned an undergraduate *and* a graduate degree, I think I am qualified, no matter what you think about my sex."

I realized later it had been even more generous than I had realized of Howard to invite Eleanor and me to the Society meeting. I deeply appreciated it. I am convinced my sex had nothing to do with the fact he never asked me again, because he often took Eleanor after that. She was the favorite sibling in our corporate family.

As patriarchs of the firm, Howard and Mel chose to control their employees because they alone knew what was appropriate for each of us within the company. They believed we were not mature enough or experienced enough or savvy enough to work without the protective umbrella of explicit instructions and timetables. In such a setting there was no room for experimentation. We were regimented carefully—even the recruiters took their orders and were expected to return to their offices and carry them out. Disagreement with company policy was not welcomed or invited.

In the beginning I had needed the controls, the careful supervision, the monitoring, the warm paternal atmosphere. It had helped me learn and become self-confident. After three years I decided it was time for a stretch and a look around. I found I wanted the authority to take risks and to be responsible in a tangible way for my actions.

Another aspect of the recruiting milieu in which we worked began to bother me increasingly, especially after my experience at the University Club. What troubled me was the sexism of management hiring practices.

Our candidates were men. Our clients were men. We found men for men. In all the time I was with the firm, we did not place a single woman in any important function. This situation existed partly because of the Catch 22 maxim which goes "you can't qualify for this job without appropriate experience and you can't get the experience because you don't have the experience to qualify."

I worked for Howard and Mel during the good old days of Affirmative Action and the Women's Movement. There was pressure on employers to hire and promote women. We would joke about it. "If only there was one who was qualified." "Find me a female with a Black mother and a Chinese father and I can get her a job anywhere, whether or not she can read or write."

The truth was, though, women were unfavorite candidates for middle- and upper-management positions. They were unfavorite candidates even if they were sharp and committed and ambitious. They were going to get married or have babies or move away if their husbands got transferred. No one takes the career of a female seriously, even in these modern days when two-family careers are in the majority of most marriages. This patronizing attitude was reflected in the subtle questions phrased in interviews. As well as asking "What does your husband do?" so you would discover the likelihood of his being transferred (although you never thought to ask a man what his wife did), you were uncomfortable with the idea of a woman traveling, holding business meetings in hotel rooms. "She'd have to get a suite with a sitting room so she wouldn't be embarrassed about the bed. It would be more expensive." There were questions about women getting to and from airports and other out-of-the-way places late at night.

Yet Howard and Mel weren't fervent anti-feminists.

Their attitudes reflected the benign and protective attitudes of American businessmen in general.

It disturbed me when I was assigned the task of locating a Group Product Manager for a consumer goods marketing department and the pool from which I was to choose—marketing departments in similar companies—contained women who seemed always to be paid less than the men in the same departments, even when their responsibilities were similar. This inequity is a severe handicap to the upward movement of women because part of the way a recruiter tells if someone is valued in their company is by examining that person's salary. If a woman is automatically paid less than a man, even when she is doing the same things, she will be thought to be inferior to the man. *If she was worth as much, she would be paid as much.*

In this search, when I brought in three people from two well-known companies, each of whom had the necessary qualifications, Mel's immediate reaction to the only woman was: "What's the matter with her? Why isn't she paid more?" That is what *everybody* thinks. That's why "equal pay for equal work" is more than a slogan. It is a necessity if women are going to get anywhere in corporations. Unequal pay is not only unfair, it prevents recognition and promotion.

Occasionally some of my old friends from Pleasantville would telephone me and we'd arrange to have lunch together. Often at these lunches they would tell me they were thinking of "going back to work" and didn't have the vaguest notion of how to go about finding a job or where they should look for one. They would ask my advice. I had become a working person so I knew.

Sometimes I helped them write their resumés. I would talk to them about how they might be able to transfer their particular interests and experience, especially in volunteer capacities, into paid work. I was struck always by the talent and capability these women displayed, invariably coupled with a remarkable lack of self-esteem. They were unable to think of themselves as worth anything except on a very narrow, limited basis. "I'm good at parties." Or, "I can make a mean pair of drapes." They needed constant encouragement and affirmation—as I once had. It was wonderful for me to realize the shoe was now on the other foot, that *I* was the one who was encouraging and helping and even counseling these women. Someplace in the preceding few years I'd learned to value my knowledge and experience to the extent that I was unselfconscious about it, I accepted my competence without having to be constantly reminded of it and complimented endlessly by my friends.

I began to formulate an idea to help women like me and my friends—housewives who wanted to return to paid work—as well as one which would give me a special *modus operandi* in the field of executive recruiting. I wanted our firm to provide a "special executive recruiting service" for our clients, one in which we would recruit qualified housewives for middle-management positions. I believed the experience gained in various volunteer positions is not only a valuable commodity transferrable to American business, I also believed that using it as leverage in the job market was "an idea whose time had come." I told Howard about my embryonic idea and he seemed interested. He gave me a green light to look into it. That was all I needed.

I found there were no corporate programs designed to welcome housewives back to the paid work force, no matter what their jobs had been before they had dropped out to raise families, no matter what the story of their achievements since had been.

Yet women run the communities businessmen live in. In this volunteer capacity, they serve as organizers and managers of most activities and aspects of life outside of the business world. They staff the local political party apparatus, run the nonpartisan voter information centers, the charitable and artistic organizations, aid and abet the schools and libraries and hospitals, manage after-school events and cultural projects—indeed are in charge of the environment itself. As I looked into the situation I discovered corporate executives had not evidenced the slightest interest in seeking, using or paying this talent. The middle-aged men's club of business was closed to middle-aged women in general and especially to housewives.

Not only was it true mature women were not part of American business management, I found, housewives in particular were not a personnel resource at all because they were outside the conventional work force. Nobody seemed to know housewives were out there, no matter how loudly and energetically they talked or waved their arms or how many communities depended on them. Communities, after all, are not businesses.

I had long ago come to the conclusion the competent management of life in the suburbs takes as much skill and intelligence as does the competent management of corporations. It is skill which can be used by business.

But how to convince businessmen of this ultimate truth? I studied the matter further.

Because the work women do in their communities is done voluntarily, the importance of that work experience is denigrated. In this world of macho sensibility, power and money are highest on the scale of values; whatever is free is of no importance. Questioning this doctrine gets you into trouble.

When women run bake sales in order to raise the money to send somebody's child to Europe to live with a foreign family (the program is called the Experiment in International Living), businessmen grin. It isn't the purpose of the fund-raising they ridicule, it is the small potatoes way in which it is done. *Bake sales,* for Chrissake. Nobody notices that, when you run a bake sale or a series of bake sales, you are running a business enterprise.

Because it is a phenomenon of human nature which requires occasional "affirmation" from others, women who run bake sales to raise money for causes, no matter how laudatory these causes may be, feel silly and unimportant. "It's only us girls running the bake sale." Sometimes it is difficult to persuade these women the skills they have developed over several years of community work are precisely the skills their husbands have been developing at their jobs. Often wives think such thoughts are disloyal and diminish the importance of their husbands' life work. I began to wonder when my friends would understand such thinking diminished their own lifework.

I spent Saturdays in the public library, studying the history of management training programs and the needs producing these programs. I found the huge growth of such programs had occurred after the Second World War, when many veterans, equipped with the GI Bill, had gone back to school, creating an enormous new demand for places in graduate schools of business. Many of these men had been integrated into business via the vehicle of "management training programs" created especially for the vets, the demand for talented new management coming because of the postwar economic boom. These well-educated vets and the carefully designed training programs created a whole new profile for American businessmen and changed forever the way business was managed. The largely entrepreneurial rugged individualist Yankee manager became the well-educated manager who depended, as an academic does, on surveys and statistics to make production and selling decisions.

What did this line of thinking have to do with my idea? It seemed that if business could accommodate an unexpected and unprecedented surge of management personnel—talented older men who were *beginners,* men who had served in the armed forces—it could surely accommodate a similar, equally talented, equally unforeseen personnel resource thirty years later: housewives who had continued to grow and learn outside of the conventional business setting for several years and who were now ready to "come in from the cold" and go to work for American capitalism as management-level wage earners. My personal discovery had been that business contained no important gender-related secrets. A smart woman had the capacity to do as well and make as valuable a contribution as did a smart man. What was lacking was the mechanism which would introduce women in substantial numbers into the business environment. I believed, as executive recruiters, we could design such a mechanism.

If we could put together a pilot package offering recruiting and business orientation training programs with carefully selected housewives as the seventies' version of the returning veterans management trainees, if we then were able to sell the concept to even one big company like Avon or Revlon or Eli Lilly or General Foods, companies with reason to court the American female because she was the principal purchaser of their products, we would be off and running. It occurred to me there was room, with this kind of service, for companies to take progressive, image-improving public stances. This seemed particularly appropriate for and needed by those companies taking a particular battering at the hands of consumers (who were mostly females): pharmaceutical companies, for example. Automobile and oil companies. Container manufacturers (remember the consumer flak about recycling?). This kind of a well-publicized campaign to recruit and use the management skills of housewives could be a terrific public relations shot in the arm for these vulnerable companies.

Moreover, I thought it was likely the project could grow to represent an exciting new frontier for executive recruiting as well. Just as recruiters know how to recruit the best and brightest men among the available male candidates, I envisioned we would recruit the most outstanding women from the sources we would develop in the world of volunteerism, a world I understood, having been myself part of it for so long. The idea pleased me most of all because it served to assuage so many of the misgivings I'd been having about executive recruiting and sexism. We would be introducing a whole new, different personnel pool to American business and, when the recruited women began to perform well, as I knew they would, the effective performance itself would serve to break down the sexist barriers.

I was excited and challenged by the idea, did a lot of studying, talked to and corresponded with people who were apt to have helpful knowledge as I planned the report. Finally, I wrote a long, carefully organized and supported proposal and submitted it timidly to Howard.

That was the end of that. It had been naive of me.

I had expected Howard would acknowledge and critique the material with me; I had worked very hard and he had indicated he was interested, at least at first. But he was always "too busy" to talk with me about it. He never discussed it, though he sometimes referred to "the woman thing" or "Sally's idea about the women," which indicated his awareness of it, if not his enthusiasm about the project.

I hadn't anticipated this response. It wasn't so much negative as indifferent. I could have argued with a negative reaction. If Howard had decided the whole idea was mad, if he didn't think the project would make money, if he thought it was too vast an undertaking for our eleven-person firm, if he thought we didn't have the specific expertise or the plan didn't fit in our long-range business plans—even if he thought housewives were too stupid to be trained for an important role in the management of American business—I would have been able to understand and to deal with his reaction. If I hadn't been able to convince him, to move him from his intransigence, well, he was the boss. He was the one, in the end, who had the right and the interest to decide such matters.

But not even to talk about it with me? Why? His reaction was something elusively different from indifference but I couldn't put my finger on it. He was aware of my continuing interest, he knew I was ready to talk it over with him, but he was skittish, nervous. I couldn't pin him down.

I thought long and hard about Howard's reaction. What could it mean? I concluded my premise had been wrong.

The veterans of the Second World War had gone off and done things other men knew about; by 1946 everybody (who was anybody) had served in the armed forces. Everybody knew all about drill, chains of command, order giving and order taking, the special language ("mess," "head"), special uniforms and different ranks, killing or being killed, bravery on the field of battle, comrades in arms, battlefield promotions, names, ranks and serial numbers. The army was a giant fraternity where men could be men and many of those veterans even today remember the war years with the rosy sentiment distance provides. They tell stories about their days in the service and meet together in groups to plan ways to celebrate and perpetuate the memory. In 1946 there was nothing invisible or unknown about returning veterans. The older men, the ones who hadn't gone to war (but wished they could have) welcomed back the returning heros by making places for them in their companies, by seeing they were able to go to school (as taxpayers, paid for it) to better prepare themselves for their peacetime roles as breadwinners and corporate executives. Since business is run on a military model anyway, there was no complicated indoctrination the veterans had to undergo upon their reentry. *They were not beginners.* They were transferring their places from one field of operation to another and there was very little dislocation in the process. Everybody who was anybody knew what soldiers did; soldiers knew what businessmen did.

But American men in this century have never known what their wives or mothers do, any more than Freud with all his insight could figure out "what women want."

This ignorance about what housewives spend their time doing is revealed when men talk about the business world as the "real" world.

If the real world is populated mostly by men, then the world populated by housewives must be "unreal," or *existing in the imagination only.*

This invisible fantasy world populated by housewives and children is a much different one from the business world of hierarchial power structures. Because it is alien, it is incomprehensible. As such, it is regarded at best with condescension and occasionally with hostility. Often we hate what we don't understand. Just as I had feared The Office and the people in it, just as I had thought they spoke and behaved there in ways alien and unfamiliar to me, so, too, do businessmen and women regard the world of housewives as mysterious and unfamiliar territory. This view has nothing to do with not enough women in management roles in companies, although that is a parallel truth. Women who have worked at any level in business for many years demonstrate the same negativism about nonpaid housewives as do businessmen. The difference doesn't seem to stem from sex but from the years of earning a paycheck. There is something the matter with you if you don't get paid for what you do, says anybody whose value is paycheck palpable.

If Howard was nervous about the special recruiting service I was proposing, he was probably no different from most other businessmen and women his age (forty-nine). If you are against an idea for emotional reasons, you will soon justify this attitude with rational arguments. That's the story of racial or sexist or any other kind of prejudice. I saw as far as Howard was concerned, my proposal covered an unspeakable topic. It was unlikely he would be willing to discuss it soon. The door was quietly and unmistakably closed in my face and once again I became an outsider.

I began to think of alternative goals for my career. I was connecting still further with my feelings and the unorthodox objectives springing from them. Now I had to ask myself a hard question: Was I ready to move on?

In 1979 nobody was offering a recruiting service providing qualified housewives for management positions in American business. It was a new idea. I considered the scary possibility of doing it by myself.

Although I was certain recruiting housewives was a good idea, I didn't know if I could do it by myself. I doubted I had yet the background or credentials to design or sell such a program on my own. It would take expert preparation and development, expert organization, packaging, and selling.

I studied the problem from as many aspects as I could think of and I talked to my friends. One day at lunch a management consultant friend listened as I described my all-over-the-park idea. Then he said,

"The recruiting service is a good idea, but in order to sell the concept you must be a recognized expert on what happens to housewives after they've gone back to work. Nobody will pay you a dime to put housewives into their companies until they know what to expect. You have to tell them. You have to know exactly what your people will do before you can market them. Having been a housewife yourself is not enough. That isn't an advantage, anyway. That's precisely what's wrong with you, what makes businessmen suspicious of you. Not only must you be able to predict accurately what your candidates are going to do, you have to demonstrate you're worth the businessman's gamble. Not only do you have to show him you're smart at business, you have to show him you understand his concerns and you know what you're talking about. Men don't know what their wives do and they would be unwilling to hire them except as servants. They might be willing to hire other men's wives if their competence could be demonstrated beyond a doubt. What you probably should do is plan to market the recruiting service in five or six years and start planning and orchestrating the project right now so you'll have the clout you need when you offer the service. That way you can achieve the status of an expert, which is what you'll need to be when you start selling the program."

This intelligent advice became the basis for Career Connection, Inc., the name of the business I incorporated as president and only employee in April 1979. The short-range purpose for my business was to counsel women who had been housewives for several years, teach them how to design and implement job campaigns, help enable them to earn job offers equal to their talents and skills. My long-range objective was the special recruiting service for companies, which would be launched when my company's files were bulging with successful case histories. In the meantime, I paid rent and postage costs by helping house-wives determine their interests and objectives, their goals and plans of action.

I planned to collect a pool of women I had counseled during their job campaigns. I would keep close tabs on these people and what happened to them after completion of the counseling, how fast they progressed in their new careers, what kinds of functions and responsibilities they handled, the kinds of difficulties they encountered which could be solved institutionally. When I was ready to market my recruiting service, I wanted to be *the* person in the field who could provide real work histories and statistics—not just theory—demonstrating returning housewives make superior middle-level managers, the major place in the business world which lacks women now. Thorough docu-mentation would authenticate the value of my recruiting program so that I could sell it as a package to companies, when it came time for that. I wanted to be able to show hard evidence that hiring and promoting such women was a sound business practice, one inviting systematization and integration into standard operations. I wanted to be able to show that reentering women made intelligent, sophisti-cated, loyal and decisive employees, that they were at least as desirable as other, more conventionally tracked employ-ees. The most intelligent, ambitious and decisive women among the women I counseled would become the pilot study group for my recruiting service. I knew they wouldn't let me down.

I began to outline the counseling service.

As an associate in an executive recruiting firm, I had participated in countless interviews. I knew what went on, where the interviewer set the traps, what the agenda was and how it was controlled and ordered. I also had learned how businesses were organized, what the purposes and *modus operandi* of the various interwoven threads of the business tapestry were, how it all fit together and what insider words and idioms were used to describe it and to participate in it.

Housewives needed as much help as they could get because they had to not only overcome the bias of the person who faced them in the interviewer's chair, they had to combat and overcome their own considerable feelings of inferiority. They had to learn the jargon and the game plans so they could start on an equal footing with their main competition, which came in two general classifications: women who had been working at paid jobs for years and had a record of substance and accomplishment, and women who were newly out of school, well-educated, fresh young things whose youthful attractiveness was a reminder of the unflinching passage of time, women who could be their own daughters, young women who forthrightly demanded the career opportunities, no matter what their educational backgrounds, that middle-aged housewives had never contemplated at that age.

At this point in history, male competition in the "judgment"-jobs market (a judgment job is one in which you must analyze something in order to reach a decision defining your next step or action; it is synonymous with "executive" position) is not nearly so important as is female competition, at least insofar as reentering females are concerned. Jobs held traditionally by men will continue to be held by men until large numbers of women work their way up and into these positions. This will happen, but it will take time. The female business-school graduates have started their steady across-the-board movement up the corporate staircase. They didn't begin to appear on the

scene in the necessarily great and unignorable numbers
until the late 1970s, however; that leaves them now still in
their twenties. Middle management (with an annual salary
between $20,000 and $40,000) is still populated, in most
fields, primarily by men. The management niches where
women have earned places for themselves, in publishing,
advertising, public relations, fields and functions where
verbal skills and the ability to deal effectively with people
are important, are open to women right now. The drag is
that because they are traditional female career possibilities,
women have to start at the bottom of the ladder and work
upwards. It is possible to get ahead in these places even if
you are a reentering female, but it takes a long time
because usually you can't start in the middle. You have to
start at the bottom, as a go-fer. You may know of
somebody's sister-in-law who started right in as Senior
Editor at *Newsweek,* fresh out of deep-frying doughnuts for
school band road trips, but she is an exception. Exceptions
prove nothing and serve only to muddy the waters of logic.

I learned the best career areas for an over-thirty-five-
year-old housewife who wants to enter middle management are jobs that are thought of as appropriate for either
sex. These are not high-stress positions (sales management, operations), but ones which are recognized as highly
detail-oriented, jobs with "administration" in their titles:
sales administration, customer service administration,
bookkeeping administration. Administration means the
same thing as management, but for some reason administrator more often means woman and manager more often
means man. There is, of course, a parallel differential in
salary.

Women my age who were still housewives didn't know
these things. They needed help, as I had needed help. Who
was out there to give them a hand? I knew they needed
custom-tailored instructions, not general advice. That
advice had little to do with returning housewives who were
involved with no recognizable careers and spent much of
their time on call for others, others whose lives would be
intimately affected by the wife-mother's departure for
outside-the-home occupations. When long-time wage
earners switch careers, no one at home is necessarily

discommoded because of the switch, since most careers take place outside the home and out of sight. Housewives are different. They have a whole load of people who are used to having them around providing services. Changing the order of the way a home is organized is a major dislocation for everyone who lives in it: There had to be ways you could make the transition easier on everybody, ways other people had figured out. Did each housewife have to reinvent the wheel when she went out looking for a job? How could the necessary information be shared?

Housewives needed data based on the empirical knowledge of other housewives. They needed hard-headed analyses of the difficulties awaiting them; they needed to know how to avoid the pitfalls and how to identify and emphasize their strong points. They needed information on the way it was in the world of business. They needed to know what to expect and how best to sell themselves out there. There was a raft of things for them to learn before they could even start a job search.

What would happen at home? What would happen at work? What actions would make it easier for their families and for themselves?

I put out my shingle and set to work.

CHAPTER THREE

The Real World

I REMEMBERED HOW IT HAD BEEN WHEN I BROUGHT our first child home from the hospital. I felt then about as capable of caring for Peter as I was able to play the clarinet. This tiny, squalling, slippery mite, who had emerged from *inside my body*, was absolutely under my care and protection. It was fantastic, amazing and scary. He didn't know I wasn't like all the other mothers because I was the only mother he had. He had no basis for comparison, as I did. *I* knew I wasn't like all the other mothers, those serene and poised persons with perfect hairdos, like Marmee in *Little Women* or Scarlett O'Hara's nameless mother, always in control, confident, expert. Every time my baby hollered, I jumped in the air and my pulse rate went to 160.

After I had been counseling for a while I began to see even the most well-turned-out of the women who came to see me shared among them this same awful secret: They didn't measure up in the world where people are paid for what they do. The business people with whom they spoke—often their husbands—didn't help much. Maureen K.'s bank-examiner husband, Ron, had told her she was "too old" (at thirty-seven) for a decent job and without sufficient experience anyway. He suggested she take the offer of a part-time job at the local library ($3.75 an hour) and forget about going into the "real" world. She came to me with big tears in her eyes, accepting what he said, hopeless, a casualty of the split-level dream: You get the house in the suburbs but your life ends.

I reminded her of something we don't often notice. Most people who give us advice about finding jobs and writing resumés, people we respect who may have fancy-sounding titles and make regular salaries, usually haven't looked for a job themselves in years. They don't necessarily know about hiring, and they don't necessarily know about looking. We take what they say as Gospel because they carry with them the aura of the world of business; actually, they don't know beans about what kinds of jobs are going to be best for experienced housewives. They don't know what being an experienced housewife means in the way of transferrable skills. More, they know little, if anything, about designing job campaigns even for themselves.

Maureen's husband was a bank examiner, not a placement officer, a hiring manager or a professional interviewer. Since he worked for a paycheck, he and she presumed he knew what was best for her if she wanted to be paid, too. The only reason for the assumption of his expertise was his twenty years in the work force. He was an expert in any aspect of the business world because he went there every day. "Real-world" reality, however, was that no matter how terrific Ron was at what he did, his boss knew better than to suddenly transfer him into the sales department or the legal department or any department about which he knew nothing and in which he was expected to use skills he had never developed. A boss understands you don't switch seasoned people out of the areas in which they are knowledgeable into areas in which they have no experience or demonstrated talent. Yet Maureen and the other women who became my clients invariably talked about their husbands, no matter what they did for a living, as if they knew best about what their wives should do in order to find a job. "Ron" or "Norman" or "Dave" knew what kinds of jobs their wives should go after, what they should say at interviews.

Plant foremen don't know about writing resumés. Vice-Presidents of Finance don't know about marketing. Bank examiners don't know about sales, which is precisely what Maureen knew about after many years of fund raising for her church, and selling was what she eventually got a paid job doing. Husbands may be loving, kind, supportive and full of fun, but they are not necessarily experts in the employment process; and not taking their advice doesn't mean you don't love them, any more than their not taking your advice in matters involving their careers means they don't love you.

In the *real* real world, the first rule of thumb is: *You know more than you think you do.*

Every time you get some advice, mull it over, ruminate on it, consider the source and whether following the advice makes sense in your particular case. Nobody knows that case as well as you, even if you've been living with somebody in holy matrimony for thirty years, even if you often brag he knows you better than you know yourself. Maybe that's true and maybe it isn't, but it certainly isn't true in the job market.

When you're looking for a paid job, your common sense must be the first line of attack.

There is an array of outside-the-home career possibilities for a woman who has been a housewife for many years. The skills a housewife has developed depend on her manner, her interests, her approach to running a household. Her special skills will dictate the jobs she will be qualified for and interested in.

In general, most housewives know how to make and meet deadlines, to set priorities, to evaluate sometimes emotion-fraught situations and come up with plans of action to resolve conflicts. A housewife is a mediator, a negotiator, a long-range planner, an expediter, a strategist, a scheduler, a market analyzer and purchaser, a motivator, a budgeter of time and money, an efficiency expert, a decision maker.

All of these skills are business skills. Each one separately is useful and desirable to people who hire people to do all kinds of jobs. Very few people who go off to work every morning and come home every Friday with a paycheck have so many different kinds of skills to offer. Few business people are experienced at keeping several balls in the air at once. That is child's play to a housewife.

Yet often the habit of asking the man of the house about even the simplest matters has become deeply entrenched and we no longer notice how dependent on him we are.

One of the things most surprising to reentering women is the statement they know better than somebody else what they want to do. They expect to take tests and classes, read books, answer questions (asked by anybody but themselves), get grades and report cards and have somebody else tell them what it is they want.

Many women in their thirties and forties—and older—believe the direction of their lives can be properly and expertly determined by an outsider.

The assumption may harken back to that last occasion when such women were "winners": grammar school. They were the ones who pleased the teacher. Their behavior was angelic, their penmanship faultless, the margins on their carefully written, perfectly spelled essays straight and true. They could add neat, tidy columns of figures in a trice, were the ones picked to read aloud, to wash the blackboard, to give out the test papers—*not* the grubby little boys who could never sit still and didn't have a clue about how to mind and do all those things so dear to the hearts of grammar school teachers. These same grubby little boys grew up to be corporation presidents.

Those little girls never had to decide what was best for them. There was always some big important person around who would make such decisions. Their job was *to obey*.

The helpless, leaf-in-the-gale person who believes somebody else knows what is best for her and can better plot her future is a direct descendant of the little girl who never ventured across the street without the crossing guard, the good little girl who walked to town with her little hand trustingly gripping the much bigger and more expert hand of her daddy. It may have appropriate then, but such dependency isn't appropriate now.

Only you can know about those actions you've taken in

your life you are proud of having taken, actions you've enjoyed and taken pleasure in. Pleasing a teacher or a counselor or a friend or your husband by telling each of them what you think it is they want to hear, what you *ought* to like or *ought* to want doesn't have a thing to do with self-awareness and goal-setting.

Obedience is appropriately left behind with hair ribbons and Mary Janes because you are the only one who can set the goals which will, in the struggle to achieve them, enlarge and enrich your life.

You must know what you're proud of having done and what you like to do before you can plan a job campaign.

Security does not beget independent thought. As long as you are comfortable in a life where you are taken care of merely because you are someone's wife or daughter or mother or "live-in" or "deduction," you don't get into the habit or the hang of independent thought and/or action. That doesn't make you a particularly good management employment risk.

You cannot have absolute security and absolute freedom at the same time. You must be willing to trade off a little of one for a little of the other until you reach a balance that suits you. When you take the responsibility for making decisions about your job campaign, when you decide not to run to your surrogate father at every unsettling juncture, that is part of the loss of protection (security) you must accept in order to achieve the independence (freedom) you want. No one else will earn a job offer for you and no one else can strike the exquisite balance between dependence and autonomy.

It is easy enough to say "pull yourself together" or "hang in there," or even "you're worth something in the job market" but these statements aren't much help when you're shaking in your boots and contemplating a leap into an unfamiliar and unfriendly terrain. Before you take that leap, it is imperative you have a deep and complete understanding of yourself as a person and as a person who is able to fit into the unfamiliar territory of the business world. You are a worker. You have been working all these years and this work has been distinctive because it is a product of your style, your intelligence and your personality.

Economists who prepare the Gross National Product statistics annually leave you out of their figures; they should remember the country's economy would fall apart if the work produced by housewives, which they ignore, vanished from the scene. Because a housewife's work is done for free, it has never been included in economic charts and graphs and forecasts. A housewife's contribution may be invisible, but it exists, and you must remember it is real work done in the real world, even if no one else does.

You must learn for yourself to translate what you have done, what you like to do and what you want to do into business lingo for your resumé and for your interviews. Then the people with whom you communicate will understand what you have to offer and you will learn what it feels like to be "one of the boys."

Marilyn M. became a registered nurse at the age of forty-three, when her two children were in college and her husband of twenty years had left her to marry the twenty-five-year-old woman who was about to have his child. It is difficult for Marilyn to maintain herself on the salary she earns as a municipal hospital nurse, so she moonlights as an artist's representative. She was home one afternoon measuring and matting lithographs for an upcoming gallery show when she heard on the radio an interview with a moderately well-known radio personality. She telephoned me to tell about it. The fellow had been talking about housewives going back to work and he characterized them as the "new immigrants." Marilyn was attracted to this approach. The phrase sounded positive and appealing, so she put down her work to listen. She paraphrased what followed:

"Returning women have no idea what the boundaries of their work are since they have not worked before in a structured environment. They're used to sitting around at home, being their own bosses and sweeping stuff under the rug if they feel like it because they know no one else cares about what they do. When they go to work in an office, they don't know what is expected of them, and they will do *anything* to please their bosses. They think their bosses are omnipotent. I always hire ex-housewives. They love me. They make me feel terrific and they work their butts off. They are like puppies, so eager they are for compliments and appreciation. They don't care what they're paid, so I can pay them anything. They don't care how hard they have to work or what hours they have to spend doing whatever it is they're supposed to do. They'll eat a sandwich at their desks and never expect to go out to lunch. Often they're bright, which is a bonus, but they're never bright about themselves. They are as easy to exploit as the immigrants at the turn of the century. I always hire housewives. I think they're terrific. I hope they never get spoiled and it's not because I'm a feminist (ha ha)."

One of the reasons women are reluctant to tackle a job search is the knowledge of people "out there" with similar attitudes. What's the use? they say. Even if we're able to convince ourselves we are smart and capable and worth some attention, Neanderthals like this one are going to lumber along and club us back to the caves. People will listen to them, not to us. We won't be able to convince anybody and we'll continue to feel like the objects they think we are.

Undoubtedly the man had his reasons for making such unreconstructed statements at three o'clock in the afternoon. He must have known most of the people listening to him were women, housewives, people who might be outraged or offended by his conceits and assumptions. If controversy breeds listeners, I reflected, the show probably had a high rating. I was not impressed with the fellow as a thinking person, however, no matter how cunningly he could play his audience, and would remember his name in case he wanted ever to run for Congress. His attitudes weren't unusual, just expressed with unusual honesty. The world is full of people who reveal their biases in the disparagement of others different from them.

I reminded myself nobody said life was easy or fair. Returning housewives *are* immigrants in the sense they are new to places their ancestors never imagined; they are on the frontiers of experience, their generation's middle-aged pioneers.

Housewives have to be smart and good at what they do in order to succeed, just like the immigrants who came before them. Smart company presidents want smart people making decisions about the future of their companies. In taking advantage of the people who work for him, the chap on the radio is not using the talent his employees have. When you waste talent, you lose productivity and ultimately you lose your profit. Smart company presidents want people working for them who can demonstrate intelligence, commitment and courage and can call these things out from the people who work for them. Prejudice and stupidity may make for entertaining radio programs but they don't make for sound business. That requires brains and that's where the future of business lies, that's why the grandsons of yesterday's sweatshop immigrants are running today's businesses. (Their granddaughters are next in line.)

Cosmetics tycoon Charles Revson once said, "A smart person can learn the business—any business—in a year. And I don't want anything to do with anybody who isn't smart."

Amen and onward.

Looking for a job is not a task for the faint of heart. Most women who have sat up all night with sick babies, who have listened for each croupy rattling tiny breath, mothers who have matter-of-factly applied cold compresses to gaping face wounds gushing blood, mothers who say "You can't go" (and stick to it) to crabby adolescents are not to be numbered among the faint of heart. Hesitation at the brink of the job search isn't a question of cowardice, it is a question of not knowing how to go over the edge before going over the edge and being frightened of not knowing.

Our son, Tom, admitted he was afraid his first day of school because he didn't know how to read.

It was, of course, *the unknown* he feared, just like many of us big shot grown-ups. We want the world to be solid, unchanging, manageable. We feel anxious when the environment seems to move beyond our ability to control it. For that reason, probably the best way to handle fear of the unknown is to look it squarely in the face. When the fear is no longer unknown and undefined, we can figure out ways to cope with it. We ask, "Just what exactly is it I'm afraid of?"

Many women have decided unpredictable, ricocheting chain reactions of change in their lives is what they most fear and can deal with least well.

Mimi L., widowed at the age of thirty-nine, put it this way:

"I've been through a lot this last year. I don't know if I can stand any more adjusting. It's like I'm a bank depositor and my checking account of adaptability is overdrawn."

Too many unwanted and unexpected things had happened to her too quickly. She hadn't had time to sort out her reactions, to shift gears into widowhood, to get used to her new identity. Now she found she was going to have to earn a paycheck in order to support herself. This was a contingency she had never before considered, and the prospect filled her with terror and made her want to run home and pull the covers over her head.

"I can get used to life without Bob," she said, "although it's hard and I still wake up sometimes thinking he's lying next to me. But I can't get used to life without *me*, the person living the life I've always lived. All this change, the new necessities and ways of looking at things have no relationship to the way I was brought up or to the expectations I had. It makes me feel like a cipher, a molecule of air in a wind storm. It's a terrible way to feel," she wailed, and she was right.

To act on one's surroundings and to resist being acted upon became the first goal of the housewife's job campaign. To disarm the overpowering nature of the job-seeking project, its vastness and complexities, it was clearly necessary to plan each step, to understand its relationship to all the other steps, and to take one step at a time. Understanding the purpose of each action and how it fit into the overall objective (landing a satisfactory job) defused the fear of the unknown.

When I was little, I learned that digging the hole to China was at least as much fun as getting there (luckily) and now I saw how important it was for reentering housewives to enjoy the process of their job campaigns nearly as much as the landing of their jobs. When you get into the habit of enjoying yourself while you're learning, life is enriched and never seems so ominous again.

It seemed to me the way to learn about what working in the business world was like in advance of working there was to design a job campaign in which the actions and strategy paralleled the activity and strategies of the business world. There are striking similarities.

Any kind of business is run with an objective. In a capitalist system, making a profit is the purpose of every business. The housewife's goal (her "profit") is to find a fulfilling job that will pay her a regular salary she is satisfied to earn. Besides being "goal-oriented," there are other correlating characteristics.

Each organizational unit within the business framework has a role to play in the achievement of the large goal—profit for the company—and for the specific goals in each specific department, which when accomplished assist in reaching the overall company goal. Like a system of interrelating gears, when you start the first one spinning, that sets the next one turning, and the next and the next, until all the gears are going and something desired is happening at the other end: a piston is being pushed up and down, for example, or, in a business, a profit is being made. Every organization depends on such a mechanism and each smaller section of the mechanism has its own corresponding purpose (gears within gears). Every job is clearly connected to other functions in its department, just as the department is connected to other departments which have other simultaneous but differing responsibilities.

There are six basic interdependent actions (connecting gears) existing in every department in a company. These same activities are reflected in the job campaign as it progresses toward its goal. Once learned, they never have to be relearned. They tell the story of an objective-related activity and each step is a logical progression.

Step by step completion of the following actions is required to complete any goal-related activity. They parallel each other in this way:

Business	*Job Campaign*

1. DEVELOPMENT

Somebody has an idea for a terrific new product, service, a modification or mutation of some existing product or service. A better mousetrap. The *developer* has the idea, tests and refines it. Hers is a creative function; she can be an inventor or a scientist (and work in the research and development department) or work in an advertising "think tank" where ideas for different advertising campaigns are generated. The *developer* works out the idea's basic skeleton.

The housewife who decides she wants to go back to paid work analyzes her background, her accomplishments and her interests—the skills which will determine her product. As a result of this examination and analysis, she *develops* the format for and the essential ingredients in her resumé.

2. ORGANIZATION

The *organizer* takes the product as identified and outlined by the developer and figures out concrete ways which will make it work. Sometimes an *organizer* is called a coordinator. She resembles the spider in the middle of the web, supervising several different activities simultaneously, acutely aware of what must be done in order to move the product along to reach the objective. She knows who should be in charge of each element of the project because she has defined and ordered the various tasks.

The housewife *organizes* her job campaign by making a list of people she knows—her contacts—by identifying, through careful research into various possibilities, the areas in which her skills will be appropriate. She defines her action steps and arranges a list of priorities. The resumé undergoes further revision and refinement.

3. ADMINISTRATION

The *administrator* sees that everybody does what she is supposed to be doing and

The *administration* of the job campaign is the ongoing accomplishment of the tasks monitors the activities the organizer has outlined. She keeps the schedules and makes the assignments. Maps with colored thumb tacks, calendars, flow charts and graphs and grids, ledgers and accounting books are all devices used by administrators to make sure deadlines are met and priorities satisfied. Administrative supervision is necessary to determine how a project is doing at any given time, whether or not activities are proceeding on schedule. An *administrator* is clearheaded, logical, detail oriented.

which have been outlined and suggested during the developmental and organizational phases. The *administrator* makes all purchases (stationery, postage stamps, books, index cards, new shoes and underwear), sets appointments and schedules, sees that baby-sitters and other home-front requirements are noticed and arranged for.

4. PRODUCTION

The *producer* makes the gadget or performs the service. Somebody else (probably the administrator) tells her how many she should make and when she should be finished. The achievement of the objective is dependent upon the fact of the product, so the *producer* has a key role.

The housewife is the walking embodiment of her experience, interests and background. She is the *product*. She *produces* her resumé (the product brochure), prepares for, arranges and participates in the interviews and all other job-seeking activity.

5. COMMUNICATION

The *communicator* must describe and explain the product. This explanation may take the form of a product manual for stereo equipment, entries in a mail order catalogue, oral or written instructions on how to put together a kitchen spice rack or installation of a battery in an automobile engine. The *communicator* may be a lecturer at a seminar, she may train

The housewife describes her background and explains her qualifications. She does this in person or in writing or on the telephone. The final resumé is a device of her role as *communicator*. It clearly explains her accomplishments. Because receiving information is an important aspect of communication, the job seeker receives and analyzes the novices in the fine art of French cooking or bicycle riding. What she does is impart information.

information the potential employer transmits as he describes the job opportunity. She understands whether it dovetails with her own requirements.

6. MOTIVATION

The *motivator* persuades people to do things they wouldn't necessarily do on their own. Salesmen are *motivators*. A good boss is always a *motivator*. The *motivator* moves the product off the shelf and into the hands of the buyer. No matter how good the idea, how thoughtfully and imaginatively packaged, no matter if the business plan has been orchestrated without a hitch, even if the product has been produced right on schedule and is ready and aching to be sold, if no one motivates a buyer to purchase it, all else is academic. In order to meet the objective—make a profit—the product must be sold. This all-important role belongs to the *motivator*.

The housewife *motivates* her potential employer to hire her through the presentation and demonstration of her qualifications. She listens carefully as the potential employer describes the position in question, she talks convincingly of her intelligence, resourcefulness and suitability in a businesslike manner. She persuades the interviewer to offer her the job.

A brief description of the six connecting actions necessary in the achievement of any objective always comes early in the job campaign. It is important to impose a coherency on the job search as soon as possible. Part of the removal of the mystery has to do with orderly definition of tasks and procedures, a recognition that only one step need be taken at a time and no step should be taken too soon or before it is comfortable.

When working on the development phase—analyzing background and skills—there is no need to be concerned or affected by the vastness of the entire project or how it should be organized or what should be said at interviews. These things come later, in their proper place.

The best way to humanize and manage a complicated effort is to focus attention on what must be done today. When you make a list of fifty things which must be done before your vacation three weeks from now, probably few of the tasks will be completed. Make a list of five necessary assignments, however, and it's likely you'll do all of them— especially if you tackle the easiest ones first. Getting a job isn't a question of turning oneself into the perfect person. That is an unrealistic goal. The world of work is full of imperfect persons, anyhow, so one's degree of perfection, or lack of it, is not a factor in the search. What a job campaign teaches, if goals are sensibly defined, are the ways to organize actions and accomplish objectives.

What is important is to get a feel for the flow taking an idea from its germination stage through to its finish. If you like to think in equations, picture the following:

$$Plan + Action\ Steps = Objective$$

One of the elements in your strategy is to demonstrate to your potential employer you are knowledgeable in the gray flannel vocabulary. When you understand every job is connected with every other job as part of the process which leads to achievement of a goal, this is called *conceptual thinking*. When you are familiar with the various tasks and distinct stages in the achievement of a goal, you are able to ask good questions about specific jobs and where they fit into the organizational *matrix* (that which gives the company or its separate departments their shape, form, structure). When you talk about goals you are talking about *management by objective*, and *that* demonstrates your ability to *think conceptually*. You learn the rules of the game through the use of its vocabulary.

Next, you must ask yourself if you want a job which challenges and stimulates you, stretches your brain and forces you to use your best and most creative thinking. That's a pressure job and the excitement of it appeals to many people. Perhaps you will perform better instead in a job which will be easy on you, where there are no particular expectations other than your steady, competent performance, a job in which you won't be threatened and where no special ambition or hunger is required, no sense of urgency is necessary.

Making these distinctions has to do with what is true for you. Perhaps you think your goal is merely to earn money. Probably your goal is more complicated than that. The *way* you earn money is a significant part of your goal. What happens at work and what your contribution there is will color your reaction to your job once you start, and whether or not you end up liking it and having it like you.

Understanding what you enjoy is important in your job search. You have to locate those responsibilities which are most similar to the kinds of things you've done in your past you've enjoyed and felt good about. Analysis of volunteer work history comes in handy here, including the kinds of projects undertaken, your style and manner of accomplishment. Sometimes your credentials look so barren only a wide-eyed optimist can see hope for the future. Actually, life is never bleak if you are able to take action. Only total paralysis is hopeless.

Mary D.'s husband had left her "to find himself." At forty-two, she had never worked for pay in her life (except teen-age baby-sitting). She was certain her life was over. She wouldn't be able to find a job, although her situation required she do so. "I'm a terrible housekeeper," she admitted. "No one would even hire me as a domestic." Mary was convinced the only reason she hadn't yet jumped from the George Washington Bridge was her ten-year-old daughter. "What will happen to her?" she kept repeating. "What will happen to her?"

She seemed in despair and as we talked, it became clear when she said she had done nothing in the last few years, it was close to being true. She had no interests outside her home. She did not go to church, had no political viewpoint, had no friends except someone from grade school who lived in a distant state with whom she corresponded. She always went to PTA meetings but was too shy ever to speak to anyone.

She was terrified at the thought of getting a job. Not only did the job-search process frighten her, the idea of going to work every day, with all the vague and haphazard concomitant terrors, filled her with dread. She was afraid it would be too much for her, more than she would be able to accomplish. We decided to concentrate on the present, to take one small step at a time and, for the time being, put off dealing with the large, menacing objective of supporting herself and her child. She made a list of things which frightened her. She confessed with embarrassment her first big fear was being interviewed by a strange man. That fear was easy enough to counter. She decided, when the time came, to locate those places in which the initial interviewing would be done by a female. Whether or not this was going to be possible was beside the point. By the time she was ready for interviews she would have been able to alter her attitude about herself and her fitness for employment. She would achieve this change by successfully completing a carefully ordered series of small action steps leading to accomplishment of each phase of her job search. She would plan and organize it carefully so no part of it would sneak up on her and turn her hands clammy in the middle of the night. She saw once she put a name on the face of her fear, the fear became manageable, even silly. She was able then to use the sensible Scarlett O'Hara dictum: "I'll think about it tomorrow." (When I'm ready for it.) This is helpful advice, one of the reasons good old Scarlett took such decisive actions. Far from being a procrastinator, she acted when she was ready to act and not before, when it was still too much for her. It wasn't time yet for Mary to worry about the interviews, that was still several weeks away. Deciding to find places where women did the interviewing disarmed that particular worry for the time being, permitted her to put it aside and allowed her to deal with today's pressing concerns.

Mary's biggest fear, the feeling that brought her daily tears and the despair which made her unable to speak above a whisper had to do with the fact she simply could not face the prospect of life without the protection and instruction of her husband.

"He told me when Jennifer should go to the dentist," she said. "He was the one who made all the appointments. He paid the bills and decided when I should have a new dress or new shoes. He told me how much they should cost and what they should look like and gave me the money to buy them."

Mary had never opened charge accounts in her name and in fact not even her house was legally hers.

She had been content with the arrangement and by the time her husband had left her, her dependence was so strongly established there was no way she could recognize the possibility of controlling her life on her own. But he wasn't coming back; she had to rescue herself.

We decided there were three critical actions she must take: She had to obtain competent legal and psychological counseling and she had to learn a trade. The psychologist at her daughter's school recommended a therapist and she was able to make an arrangement wherein she did typing at home to pay for her visits. The local chapter of the National Organization for Women recommended her to a lawyer who was sympathetic and experienced in dealing with women in her situation.

Next, Mary obtained a position as a file clerk in a local insurance agent's office. That wasn't too hard to do—the pay was low and the work so boring it fit in with her dismal outlook about herself. Since she already had been acquainted with the woman in charge of the office, she hadn't had to worry about the interview.

I pointed out there was evidence she was a responsible person and when she demurred, I noted she had always attended PTA meetings, even though she had never had the nerve to speak to anyone. She was surprised and reluctantly agreed with me. "Yes, I am responsible," she said with quiet surprise. "I've never thought about myself in that way before."

She enjoyed doing the kind of quiet, tenacious work legal research requires, so working in a law office seemed a fine idea. She enrolled in a night school for paralegal training. As a paralegal, she would perform a task-oriented function: She would receive the assignment from the attorney in charge, go off, do it, return with the completed task and receive her next assignment.

This was a satisfactory solution for this particular woman. Mary required an ordered regimen and the imposition of an authority's affirmation of her performance. Both of us were pleased when she pulled herself together and did all of the things she had to do. She did not sit home licking her wounds and feeling sorry for herself, although that was tempting behavior for a dependent person who was used to others running her life. She behaved thoughtfully and with courage and she took action. The last time I saw her she looked her age instead of ten years older. Needless to say, her daughter is proud of her.

Important truths to keep in mind, no matter how desperate the situation, how unsuited you think you are to taking charge or how few choices are open to you:

You can get help.

There are always choices.

Sometimes the options are loathsome: admitting failure and moving in with your parents or the sister-in-law to whom you haven't spoken since your cousin's wedding. There is public assistance for people who are in deep trouble, as well as private charities.

If you can't type, learn to type (everybody should know how, including corporate presidents). While you're learning, there are jobs like waitressing, baby-sitting, cooking and cleaning for others, filing and general office work. These jobs are always around and if your situation is desperate you can do any of these things or think of others.

Pride and desperation make a ridiculous combination. Remember no one cares as much as you do about your reputation, or what the neighbors will say about what you've fallen to. Taking care of yourself and your family, earning your self-respect, must remain the primary consideration. In addition, and very important, unless you live on Bikini Atoll, there are people around you and many of them will be willing to assist you if you are in need. Camouflaging your situation serves only to make you more frantic and wastes time anyway. Sooner or later, when your shameful secret (whatever it is) is revealed, and it always is, you will look much more pitiful than you would have had you been forthright. You want to take care of yourself, not have people feel sorry for you.

You will not die. Wounded pride or diseases stemming

from punctured-image are rarely fatal. Starvation is, but starving to death in your situation is unlikely. Face the worst possibility you can think of—the bank will foreclose the mortgage—and figure out what you are going to do *then*. Weeping and carrying on is fine for the movies but quite silly in real life. You are in charge of getting on with your life, even if your heart is broken. The sooner you take action, even if it is the wrong action, the better you feel and the more likely the next action will not be a mistake. (Do not invest your money in a harebrained scheme just now.)

The important thing is to get moving.

PART TWO

A Handbook
For Housewives

CHAPTER ONE

Narrowing It Down

YOU HAVE DECIDED YOU ARE GOING TO LOOK FOR A paid job. You feel older than anyone else, uncertain, inexperienced. You don't know how to proceed.

Use this primer as a road map. It will show you the landmarks, the twists and curves, the various routes enabling you to reach your destination. Because you are in the driver's seat, the journey to your job will be more comfortable, less surprising and far more enjoyable than it would have been if somebody else was steering the car and making all the decisions for you.

The basis of all good advice must be practical. Advice must fit in with reality, possibility and workability. Otherwise, any well-meant counsel hovers around the edges of fantasy and "if only." When you're looking for a paid job after you've been working for many years without pay, you must require sensible understanding of yourself and your ambition to guide your job search. In order to do this successfully, *you must understand what works for you before you can do anything about working for anybody else.*

What works for you may not work for the woman down the street. That doesn't mean one of you is inferior to the other. It merely means you are different. In addition, you don't have to prove you love your mother by imitating her life. What was right for her may or may not be right for you. It's up to you to decide.

You Must Pick Your Place

Women often say to me: "Picking my place in the job force is a luxury. I have to find a job, anything, get hired and somehow *then* I'll see if I can do it, or if I like it. Job satisfaction is the last thing on my mind."

Very few situations are that desperate. Even if you accept the first offer that comes along, time doesn't stop at that moment. You will be learning, experimenting, trying different things every day. Jobs always take on the profile of the personal style of the persons within them, even the most routine and unimportant jobs.

If you hate the work you do, your hate and unhappiness will show and you will do your work poorly. This assures one of two things: either you will be fired, or you will never get out of doing what you loathe. Either possibility is unacceptable. You will not be rescued, so you'd better address the problem before it happens, when you can still avoid it. *Nobody ever got promoted for doing a poor job.*

Don't be too quick to call the necessity of imposing choice on your options a "luxury." Taking responsibility for your actions means weighing and analyzing the possibilities open to you *before* you commit yourself. Children are impulsive, require instant gratification and rarely give thoughtful consideration to the consequences of their actions. They tend to leap before they look, which is the *real* luxury, something you, as a grown-up, recognize as ill-conceived and unjustifiable behavior.

More, it is much harder to go about the business of looking for another job when you are working already. The time you can devote to interviews is restricted, you cannot make or receive telephone calls, you can't organize the project as it should be organized. A job search is a full-time job in itself.

Surprisingly enough, as a housewife who has not had a paying job in many years, you are at your strongest negotiating point *right now*. The moment you accept a position with a salary, that means a promotion, a transfer, even a new job and certainly a raise will be based on that salary. If you take the first job offer that comes along, probably it will pay much less than you are worth and far less than you want or need.

So don't rush toward the paycheck just because it's there. Taking four or five months in the search process may mean several thousand dollars to you in the long run.

Talking Turkey

While we're talking about money, let's enlarge upon the subject and talk about what makes a business tick.

Businesses exist to make money. In order to make money, each company sells a product or service (for the sake of clarity, we will assume service and product are synonymous). Often other companies are involved in selling the same kind of product. When that happens, the companies are in competition with one another. Each company tries to do something better than its competition so customers will prefer to buy its product: It may lower its prices, improve its product one way or another, make sure people recognize its name more quickly or with a more positive attitude than they do those of its competitors. Every year all the sales in dollars of all the companies selling the same category of product are totaled (all the automobiles, for example, or all the hair-coloring products). The portion of that total one particular company's product has is called its *market share*.

Companies are always trying to enlarge their market share; much of their business planning has that objective.

A company's internal workings are devoted to the production and sale of its product. Jobs which are directly concerned with making the product or selling it are called *line* jobs. These jobs have a direct relationship with the company's income.

For example: In the Ivory Soap Company, the plant manager is in charge of the vats and the ingredients that go into the vats (whatever the soap is made of); he supervises the supplies to see there is always a sufficient amount available to continue production. In addition, he sees that the temperature in the vats is kept at the proper soap-making levels and the mix is always identical; in other words, he controls the quality of each of the batches. He is also in charge of overseeing the people on the assembly line who cut the hardened soap into neat little squares and feed them into the packaging machinery, boxing the properly wrapped bars of soap into crates and loading the works into trucks ready for shipment. The plant manager's job is a *line* job. When he needs to hire a person to be in charge of *quality control* he may call the personnel manager and give him a *job order:* "I want a quality control manager who is experienced in soap making." The personnel manager and the quality control manager are both *staff*, not *line* positions. They are not *line* because they are at least one step removed from the manufacture of the product.

Manufacturing, operations, sales are *line* functions. They are directly involved with the product. Other jobs (personnel, public relations, bookkeeping, advertising) are *staff* functions. They support the *line* but are not directly responsible for profit and loss *(P and L)*. Because of the close relationship line jobs have with the company's profit, they are more prestigious. The people who hold these positions are paid more money, both in terms of salary and other important benefits, like the opportunity to buy stock in the company at discounted rates. Line jobs are rewarded well because the people who hold these jobs take greater risks than the staff people. Their jobs are literally "on the line" because the decisions they make either improve or damage the company's P and L. Everyone else "down the line" can see the results, too. When a sales campaign bombs, the sales manager is fired (unless he is the son-in-law of the company president, in which case he will be *moved upstairs* or given a *special project*). There is something clean and attractive about immediate results. Maybe that's why people have been drawn to business for so long: It is so lacking in mystery, so straightforward. Nothing is as obvious as an annual balance sheet announcing the success or failure of company management. It is the ultimate report card.

Banks, insurance companies, public relations agencies

all have ultimate concern with the income which produces their profits. All of them contain line and staff jobs, even though their products are service or support oriented.

Staff jobs are usually more secure than are line jobs, probably because mistakes in them are not so quickly apparent. These jobs don't reflect directly on company profits, anyway. The truism about security and freedom still exists: The more risk taken, the more interesting (and vulnerable) the job is; the less risk taken, the more boring (and safe) the job probably is.

Although more line people get to be presidents of companies, more jobs within companies are staff jobs. You can surmise from this that most businessmen have staff personalities. Line jobs produce the leaders; both are necessary to the running of the company, it's just in hierarchial structures, the generals always get the glory.

Because a staff job is outside the *profit center*, it is not considered to be a *decision-making*, or *judgment* job and as such, no one with any salt would want it. That is nonsense, of course. There are all kinds of decisions to make in staff jobs, but the prejudice exists and fits nicely within another cherished inaccurate belief. Most housewives believe they have held a nondecision-making job for years (outside the profit center and, therefore, definitely inferior). For this reason they feel additionally insecure when they enter the job market. They forget to remember *stereotypes are rarely accurate*.

When a housewife starts looking for a paid job, she may look for a second-string kind of a job because the housewife stereotype is one in which she serves another. The job-hunting housewife looks to become something similar—a secretary, an administrative assistant, a researcher who is not permitted to analyze, a writer of speeches somebody else delivers.

Perhaps a support job will be best for her. Perhaps not. She won't be able to discern the truth as long as she permits the role-playing to interfere with her self-knowledge. As long as she is playing the stereotypical role of housewife, she is talking *should* and not *is*. She is guilty of blatant stereotyping and she is her own victim.

Finding out what she does most comfortably leads to

the achievement of the first objective in the job campaign, which is to define her *ideal job.*

What this does is gives her necessary self-awareness and compells movement in the direction of a job requiring her unique experience and special style.

Describing Your Ideal Job

Most companies have forms, called *job descriptions,* for department managers to fill out. Each position under the manager's purview has such a *description.* Whenever somebody is interviewed for a specific job in that department she receives a *job description,* so she knows what is entailed and whether or not she's interested.

What you will be doing is writing *your* job description, using the knowledge you have about yourself and how you can expect to fit into a business setting. You don't have to know anything about business to write *your ideal job description.* What you have to know about is what you like to do.

1. What do you like to do? Most women have told me the thing they like to do best is to "deal with people." As many women have told me "I'm good with people" as have told me "I can't do anything." Often the same women make both statements. (It is curious that working with somebody else is not "doing anything.")

Although not everyone claims an ability to deal with people, many housewives do, so let's start there. "Dealing with people" is much too broad a phrase to be helpful in the writing of the *ideal job description.* Everyone deals with people at some point during the week. Contact with other people cannot be avoided. Dealing *well* with people is an attribute, certainly, but the phrase still doesn't describe how it is accomplished, under what conditions and what specific purpose or orientation is served by the contact, or "dealing well."

Here is a place for some careful, detailed and detached thinking. Remember you are not making judgments about whether the things you like are good or bad things to like. They are the things you enjoy.

2. How do you do what you like? When you "deal with people," the first step is to make contact with the other person. How do you prefer to make contact? Telephone? In person? Through a letter, or with an intermediary? Do you tend to have conversations with people in line at the supermarket, or are you more formal? Do you like to warn people you are about to contact them rather than just walking in on them "cold"? (A "cold" telephone call is used by salesmen and reporters.) Do you like to make the overture or do you prefer to wait until the other person makes contact with you? Are you shy before meeting people, then warm up quickly when you're with them?

Answers to these questions will help determine not the quality of your interaction, but your *style*. Understanding the personal style you impose on your relationships with other people will tell you what areas of the business world you will feel most comfortable in. For example, a salesperson sells. What she does in order to sell is *motivate* and *persuade*. She is able to talk somebody into doing something they don't necessarily want to do. Such an objective can be reached by the most blatant of arm-twisting *(a hard sell)* to the gentlest, most subdued conversation which barely touches upon the issue at hand *(a soft sell)*. Her personal style will affect the way the encounter goes, but it will not change the objective. In this encounter, the objective is *to persuade* and *to motivate*.

Many women who are "good with people" recoil from the sales role. They characterize themselves as "good listeners": "People like to talk to me, to tell me their problems." These people's personalities don't demand center stage, necessarily; rather, they feel comfortable when the other person is talking, when they are silent. Their purpose is *to receive*.

People who *interview* are *receivers*. They may ask questions and direct the conversation, but their primary interest and responsibility is *to receive* information from another person.

Some people like to be in situations where other people seek them to ask advice. They like to help other people through difficult situations by suggesting behavior. The personal style in this instance includes anything from actual *commanding* (officers in the military service *command* their troops; so do officers in any authority-based structure), to the offering of gentle suggestions. The objective here is *to advise*. All kinds of counseling jobs exist, ranging from ones which require years of schooling to those with relatively short training periods. The people in them, however, are there because they like *to advise*.

Still other people like *to seek advice*. They aren't comfortable making decisions until they have sought and received the counsel of others. This assists them in making whatever decisions they make. On the surface, this behavior may seem indicative of a passive personality, but that's not necessarily so. Think about it. Seeking information, even biased information (opinion), as long as it isn't reflective of a pathological uncertainty, represents a legitimate personal style. The goal of this kind of interpersonal encounter is *to find out*.

Researchers collect data *to find out*. So do *reporters*, people who make *surveys*, *scientists*.

You can see that "dealing with people" has many possibilities for personal variation. It is up to you to decide which of the countless possibilities seems appropriate to your personal style. What makes sense for you?

Once you have made a statement about what you like to do ("I like to deal with people"), you must then ask yourself, "How do I prefer to do it?" We've seen the answer can be stated in the infinitive form of one—or many—action verbs. This unusual way of answering the questions, How do I go about doing what I like to do (what is my personal style)?, springs from my understanding of how actors construct their approaches to the parts they play. An actor must become aware of his character in the same way you must become aware of yourself. The tools he uses in his task are tools useful to you. The difference is that the actor is intellectually constructing a person outside of himself, who may or may not resemble his own personality; you are constructing, or coming to know better through reflection and rigorous honesty, the person *you really are*.

Let me explain briefly what an actor does so you can see

why it works as well for someone who is defining career objectives.

An actor must know the objective for every scene in which he appears. This helps him know the objective of every encounter within each scene. The *objective,* and all the actions leading to its achievement, can be defined by using the infinitive form of the pertinent verb.

For example, in a whodunit, the detective comes into a room full of people, all of whom are suspects. The detective knows (but the audience doesn't) which one of the people present is the murderer. He will tell the story of the crime to the assembled group, building dramatic tension as he goes along and climaxing the scene by identifying the killer. Depending on the actor's interpretation of the scene and the personality of the character he is playing, his objective for the scene is *to reveal* or *to accuse.* You can see the ways the scene might be played will be different from one another, even though the dialogue is the same in either interpretation; the way the scene is played depends on the objective.

During the buildup toward the objective, there are actions the actor selects which point toward it. He might want to *disarm* the suspect (and thus the audience) if his objective is *to reveal,* so the murderer (and the audience) will be surprised by the revelation; he might, therefore, smile at the suspect or touch him in some seemingly innocent and trusting way, in order *to disarm.* This way he will insure the climax *(to reveal)* will be a real surprise to everyone.

If the actor has decided the objective of the scene is *to accuse* (a much more overtly aggressive objective than is *to reveal*) he will design the actions in the scene leading up to the climax in a way suggesting aggression. He may choose *to threaten* or *to menace* and will use his posture or the stage props to do so. For example, swinging a fireplace poker like a golf club can be a covertly menacing device suggesting the scene's objective, in this case, *to accuse.*

All of this talk of actors' techniques serves to illuminate the ways you can construct a methodology of actions which will assist you in reaching the objectives you have selected for yourself. If your objective is "to deal with people" some of the actions you are going to take to reach that objective may be *to teach, to convey information, to guide.*

When your objective is identified, you will then list a whole set of actions affecting the way to meet that objective, just as actors do. There are many possibilities if your objective has to do with dealing with people. They are all dictated by you and what you decide is important to you, the ways most appropriate to your behavior and feelings. Some of the actions you might decide to take could include *to advise, to seek advice, to lead, to nurture, to support, to tell stories, to teach.* There are a million action verbs which might serve. Some will apply to you and the way you interact with others, others will be all wrong for you. You decide.

3. *Where do you like to do it?* So far, we have asked two questions: What do I like doing? and How do I like to do it? The next questions is, Where do I see myself doing it?

Setting is important to you. It has to do, first of all, with the ideal geographic location of your job. If you can drive and have regular access to a car, then distance from your home may not be as important as it would be if you are dependent on the bus or other public transportation. Time spent in getting back and forth is an important consideration because you know what must be done before you leave in the mornings and after you get home at night. An hour's travel time is too much if you have other major and time-consuming chores. On the other hand, an hour's commute may be precisely what you want in order to read the paper, write letters or look out the window and relax. (I require looking-out-the-window time during the day, for the time and privacy *to ruminate* is one of the requirements of my ideal job.)

Besides geographic location, *setting* also has to do with the room in which you do your work. Perhaps you see yourself in an office with people scurrying around, typewriters clacking and telephones ringing. Or in an office which appears, in your mind's eye, to resemble a library more than a place of business. Bookshelves, carpets, people who speak softly and seldom.

Perhaps you want to work in your own home. Say so! When you start your job campaign, you can decide which aspects of your *ideal job description* you are willing to modify and which aspects you feel strongly about. Right now the only requirement is clearly spelling out exactly what it is you want.

4. *When do you like to do it?* Next comes *when*. Is your ideal job nine-to-five, Mondays through Fridays? Most jobs are. Some people, however, despise the notion of regular and conventional work schedules. If you're one of these people, take note of it. This knowledge limits the areas in which you can make a decision, and knowing that is helpful to you. (If you have said you prefer working at home, then you probably also said you prefer to mandate your work hours; one follows the other naturally.)

5. *How much money do you want?* Be sensible, not apologetic or out of left field when you talk about money. Of course everyone would like to make $100,000 a year, but that is not a practical answer when you are out looking for your first paid work in a long time. (Give yourself a couple of years to reach that goal.) Figure out how much you *need*. If you are the sole support of your household, total all the fixed monthly costs (rent or mortgage payments, taxes, electricity and telephone, insurance, food, loan payments, heating, transportation, etc.). To this figure add other costs that vary from month to month: house maintenance (painting, plumbing and other appliance attention), entertainment, doctor bills, clothes, car costs like gas, oil and repairs, vacation, etc. Add both lists together and multiply the total by 15 percent (.15). That is what you need to live on and if it looks like a lot of money, it is. We are living in a different world from the one we inhabited twenty years ago. The poverty level is anything under an annual income of approximately $8,000—and what single person can live on that, much less take care of a family?

Twelve thousand dollars a year doesn't sound like much when you look at it this way, does it? Money is always a big battle when you're negotiating with a potential employer. Remember this maintenance figure and don't budge from it. You cannot afford to take less unless you are willing to change the way you live, and that's something you may have to address sooner or later. For now, for your ideal job, stick to the way you live right now and the amount of money required to continue that current standard of living.

If you are not the sole support of your household, you may not need as large a salary. If you understand the inflation rate is hovering around 12 percent, you may figure what was adequate bacon this time last year isn't enough by the time this year rolls around. (That's why you added 15 percent to your total living costs.) Unless your name is Rockefeller or Vanderbilt, your family probably needs the money your second income is going to bring into the house.

If, however, your name *is* Rockefeller or Vanderbilt, and you don't need the money you will earn, then relax. Money is not the motivating force compelling your move in the job market. You're a lucky lady.

Writing Your Ideal Job Description

Conventional *job descriptions* are divided into three parts:

1. Responsibilities
2. Preferred Personality
3. Compensation

Your *ideal job description* will closely resemble the ones used by businesses, at least insofar as it is organized (otherwise it will be better: clearer, more to the point, definite).

1. Responsibilities. When you have chosen the action verbs which best fit the way you want to reach your objective ("I want to deal with people; I want *to talk, to listen, to interpret* what the other person tells me; I want *to give advice*"), decide which of the six general categories of goal-achieving skills (development, organization, administration, production, communication, motivation) your action steps fit into (See Chapter 3, Part I). For example, if you are comfortable giving advice to people, you may have developed *motivational* skills. If you want *to sew, to make clothes, to knit, to construct* cribs and bookcases, you want to work in *production.* If you want *to reflect, to create,* or *to solve problems,* you are interested in *development.* Actions fitting under the umbrella of *assigning, scheduling, following-through* are *administrative* skills.

A specific job has certain responsibilities which differentiate it from every other job in an organization. You have been outlining what you like and how you like to do it. Now it is time to transfer this knowledge into business vocabulary. Don't panic. None of the words will be words you don't know. It is just that the language is more formal than you're used to. The reason for this is you must learn to take your ability and your ambition seriously. Proper language will help you do that.

Here is a person who said she likes "to deal with people." Under *Responsibilities* she has put:

My skills are *motivational.*

A major part of the time will be devoted to interaction with people in order *to persuade* and *motivate* them to purchase my company's product. This will be accomplished through discussions on the telephone and follow-up, in-person visits. Initial telephoning and record keeping will be done at my home with time and work load restrictions set by me.

(This is a classic method of performing sales on commission.)

Or

My skills are *motivational.*

Much of my work will focus on interaction with people in order *to persuade* and *motivate* them to purchase my company's product. This will be accomplished by my *visiting* and *talking* to potential buyers, *demonstrating* the quality of my offering by *displaying* and *discussing* carefully *documented* support material such as brochures, charts, audio-visual set-ups, etc. I will work in an office which will be located within a fifteen-minute walking radius of my home.

(Many women who have done fund-raising for private charities have used such supporting material—prepared either by themselves or by their organizations. Companies do the same thing. They call these displays "marketing" or sales presentations. School teachers do this stuff every day.)

* * *

You don't have to give reasons for anything in your *ideal job description*. You are describing the optimum conditions under which you will work and the perfect responsibilities. Modifications and compromises occur only when you fully understand what you want. For example, a two-and-a-half-year-old child has to learn his toys belong to *him*, will be returned to him because they are his, before he can share them. That's why a two-year-old will scream bloody murder when you ask him to share things with nice little Joey from down the street. He doesn't understand yet they belong to him. Two or three years later, he will have progressed through that developmental phase and will comprehend the concept of private property. So, too, you. Modifications and compromises in your job plan occur only when you understand and accept what you want.

> I have *communications* and *developmental* skills.
>
> An important part of my job will be interaction with other people, at which time I will *ask* questions relating to some aspect of my responsibility which is *to collect* data, *to write* reports; I must *interview* people whose knowledge is used in the compilation of the information necessary in writing the report.
>
> (This person wants *to write* and *to do research* in order to achieve her objective of "dealing with people." See how both actions can fit in her effort to reach her goal?)

Besides "I like to deal with people," other frequently named preferences include "I like to write," "to read," "to talk," "to analyze," "to evaluate," "to think." The important thing to remember is businesses are designed and populated by human beings and you are a human being. Therefore, the jobs within companies will have responsibilities which people like you possess. Assignments and responsibilities exist which are right down your alley—*now*. A job search is a matchmaking exercise. The responsibilities you will be assigned when you accept a job offer will reflect your interests and ability *if* you have been honest with yourself in defining the things you like to do and have been able to demonstrate and transmit that information to your potential employer.

2. *Preferred Personality.* The part of a job description which follows the *Responsibilities* section usually talks about the kind of personality characteristics that best fit the already described *responsibilities.* Favorite business phrases going in here are "self-starting," "goal-oriented," "aggressive" (code word for male), "articulate." I have yet to see a *preferred personality* section of a job description including words and phrases like "has to be pushed to start," "confused," "timid," "inarticulate." You can see not much thought goes into the adjectives used in the conventional business *personality profile* because the words used are always the same. That's why verbs are so much more significant. You can't afford the luxury of sloppy thinking which presumes every success story is the result of a handful of adjectives, no matter what the job. Success is a result of taking *appropriate action.*

Decide what parts of your personality cause your interests to spring forth. For example, if one of the things you like to do is "to talk," then it can be presumed you are articulate. You are articulate when you tend to think in a well-organized way so the stories you tell have a beginning, middle and an end, or if you are often able to convince someone to your point of view or to describe it in a way that satisfies you.

Many jobs require people who use language well, who are able to explain an idea or to convince someone to a particular point of view. These are jobs requiring *communications skills.* Communications skills have become a big deal since the 1960s. If you like *to talk,* then your *preferred personality* section will include those attributes you recognize in yourself which make you a good talker. Some of these may include a good vocabulary, a pleasant speaking voice, an ability to think clearly and logically. Or to hold people's attention (that could come from a high energy level or a sense of humor).

If a preference of yours is *to read,* a whole set of other characteristics crops up, some identical, as a matter of fact. A reader has to have a good vocabulary too, but doesn't need to have a pleasant speaking voice (unless you like *to read aloud*) or necessarily the capacity for logic. Probably, a reader must have tenacity—an ability to stick to something even when it is a large or formidable task. In addition, someone who reads is content to be stationary for long periods of time, probably likes quiet surroundings and has an active imagination. There are other, subtle things about readers, too. Reading, like talking, is the skill of a person who understands the importance of language, but it is also visible evidence of education, or a desire for it (unlike talking). Some people like to brag they read "a book a week," not because they respect the material they've read, but because they respect the act itself. There is sometimes an element of snobbery or elitism in people who like to read and it is important to understand that, because this, too, has important ramifications on the direction of your job search.

What about people who don't like *to talk* or *to read?* What about people who like *to drive,* or *to build,* or *to fix,* or *to make?* Each of these actions requires a specific set of personality characteristics. A driver, because her skill is dependent on eye-motor coordination, is probably quick, active, decisive. Language skills, other than the ability to read and interpret road signs and maps, aren't nearly so important. Reflective characteristics aren't necessarily present in people like this, although, of course, anything is possible and some people like *to read* and *to build.*

The point of the *preferred personality* section of the *ideal job description* is to provide a vivid, clear picture of the person you are by describing the way you behave when you fulfill the responsibilities you want.

3. *Compensation.* Management salaries are always described in annual salary figures. Lowly secretaries and clerks talk about how much they make a week and blue-collar workers talk about hourly wages.

You can write your salary requirements in a single sentence, using the formula worked out earlier. In a job description, the compensation is usually figured to reflect two separate realities: What the customary dollar value is for the job described in *responsibilities,* and how the job relates to other jobs in the company, peer jobs, superiors' jobs, subordinates' jobs.

You aren't able to do this since you have no way of

determining these things. So you will merely tell what your requirements are.

Summing Up

When you have decided what the things you like to do are, you may have listed some of the following words: *To read; to talk; to listen; to write; to find out; to teach; to fix; to paint; to type; to cook; to watch; to play chess* (which uses developmental and organizational skills).

Your *responsibilities* section could read as follows:

My skills are in the area of *communications.*

Using my interest in reading and language, I will *select* and *study* material which will help me *to write* documents. I will *prepare* this material in written format as well as in the form of oral reports, which I will *present.* I will *describe* the steps used in reaching my conclusion and will *discuss* the merits of this conclusion.

This paragraph describes fairly precisely what it is that a documentary writer does; so, too, a marketing or advertising strategist, a person whose responsibility it is *to communicate ideas.*

Your personal style is appropriate to many functions. The issue isn't that you've proved you can do *anything,* in *any* function, quite the contrary. You have limited your opportunity by focusing on your strengths—what you *can* do. If you are offered a job where you are required to add columns of figures all day or to spend forty percent of your time on the telephone asking questions on a checklist prepared by some other unknown person, you'll know whether that job is or isn't for you.

It isn't necessary to know the title of the job you're going to have ("Product Manager" or "Project Leader" or "Pool Supervisor"), but it is necessary to know the skills you bring to it.

One of the women with whom I worked wrote the following under her *preferred personality:*

* * *

Self-educated, reflective, impatient with exaggeration or undocumented arguments, stubborn, willing to work long hours to complete a project, curious, always asking 'why?' and 'how come?,' comfortable with deadlines, intense.

She has a good grasp of her personality because not all of the words she has selected are complimentary to her, but they are all important. She has an idea of where she will end up and where she will feel most comfortable, even though she doesn't know the title under her name or where her desk will be placed. These are things she can find out later.

The information she has organized in her *ideal job description* is for her eyes only. That is important if she is to permit herself to be truly honest.

Every job search must begin with self-knowledge. If you require honesty from yourself, the chances are good you will hit the ground running.

CHAPTER TWO

Resources

Making Contacts (Networks)

Since there is no such thing as a new human need, only different ways of expressing old ones, the study of language is a useful way to examine what people are thinking about at different times. When certain words become fashionable, their usage reveals people's preoccupations and conceptions, their feelings about one another and the eternally shifting focus of society.

I remember in the 1960s *polarize* was a popular word. It was a tidy way to describe what was happening when teenagers and their parents seemed to face each other across a chasm of distrust and misunderstanding. Although it was widely used, the word wasn't particularly accurate because *polarize* carries a distinct impression of entrenchment and hardening of opposing positions, contrary to what, we see now, was actually happening in the sixties, when movement and changing attitudes, and not polarization, were the norm.

Memory of the word's prominence in the popular commentary shows how easy it is to mistake shorthand evaluation of a situation for truth, which brings me to another currently popular word, *networking*.

I don't think much of nouns when they masquerade as verbs and I don't think much of using the word *network* when you mean the people you know and the people they know. Use of the word to mean this is a fad, and it will go away as all fads do. I will welcome its quick disappearance, because I believe the current use of the word dramatically oversimplifies a subtle, shifting story of relationships between people. In addition, and this is the major bugaboo with career housewives who feel themselves outside the action, in the shadows and without measurable value, the word is frightening in a creepy way because it serves to isolate people who already feel themselves outsiders. The use of this particular word to describe an age-old method of giving and receiving favors has sprung up during this age of technology and it imposes an electrical, impersonal quality on personal relationships. It makes you think of wires and television sets and circuits so tiny you have to repair them with special miniature tweezers. It doesn't make you think of old friends and long-standing, comfortable relationships. It makes you want to click and squint and flash on and off.

Let's put aside that use of the word when we mean a group of people with whom you are acquainted who themselves are acquainted with other people.

Your Friends

Your friends are a major resource in your job campaign. Don't force relationships into impersonal categories by referring to them as a *network*. You want to feel warmly about your friends so you can talk with them honestly and so you will be able to ask them for help, something with which friends and other kinds of acquaintances feel comfortable but electrical gadgets don't.

If you have worked in politics, you know the practical value of doing favors. Do one for somebody, and one day when you need something, it will be reciprocated. You have to ask for what you want. You don't presume people can read your mind. In politics people rarely do things out of a spirit of generosity and good fellowship. In a legislative body—the playing field of politics—philosophical agreement, at least on a day-to-day basis, is not nearly so important as getting support. Politicians never hesitate to ask favors of one another, sometimes very big favors, because it is part of the game and asking and giving are of equal importance.

You may have noticed there aren't a whole lot of women on the national political scene. The reason I point this out is the political instinct for reciprocity ("You vote for the dam in Mississippi, I'll vote for the workers' program in Detroit") is something quite alien to many women. Middle-aged women hate asking favors, even from each other. Yet they are generous and kindhearted when somebody comes along and asks a favor of *them*. You figure it out. It is as if it were bad to ask somebody to do something for you but good to do something for somebody else. Since both actions are part of the same process, how can one be so much better than the other?

"Oh, but I feel terrible asking Nancy. She's so busy. I'll just be adding to her burden. Besides, *I should be able to do it myself.*" Women suppose they must do things themselves. The rugged individualists of the twentieth century are its women. In the last century, the idea of the rugged individualist (a male) was the pioneer who took his family to the outskirts of civilization, cleared the land and asked and received no help. No government intervened in his task, no reward was expected except personal satisfaction and the dignity of virtue.

Today, women are the rugged individualists who do everything themselves or else think they are shirking their duty. This may be due partly to the fact women didn't grow up learning they were part of a larger whole (except in Sunday School). Little girls were taught history and science and math and English and nothing whatever about the economics of a household, instruction in nutrition, purchasing or human psychology. (Home Ec taught how to make chocolate pudding from scratch.) There was no instruction having to do with how running a household fit in with society's other functions. Women were on their own. There was no pie-shaped graph in the Social Studies textbook dividing national production into categories like agriculture, manufacturing, distribution, professional services and household support. What women did in their homes was never thought of as being part of any larger whole, it was an end in itself and totally separate from other homemaking centers. There lay inherent within the function no aspects of cooperation or connection with other segments of society. It had nothing whatever to do with being a member of a team. Not expected to perform on a team, girls' gym classes had us doing calisthenics and exercises, modern dance and gymnastics, playing basketball with stupid rules preventing anybody from taking more than three steps at a time. When we played field hockey, it was for the purpose of running around outside and getting color in our cheeks; there were no strategy sessions, we weren't *coached* to understand "plays" to perform in tandem with one another. Not trained to act as a member of a team, we ended up not knowing what part of the whole thing was our responsibility. We believed *everything* was our responsibility—at home, anyhow. Outside our front door, nothing was our responsibility.

Linda S.'s husband has been unemployed for seven years, since his small printing business went bankrupt. She plans and cooks every meal and is in charge of seeing the laundry is done and put away, the rugs shampooed, the couch slipcovered and the windows washed—even though he stays home and she goes to paid work every morning! She has never said to him, "Look, you're home all day, it makes sense if you take charge of the household." Perhaps she feels his vanity will be injured if he sees she has noticed the change in his situation. For whatever reason, she has opted to continue doing both the breadwinning and the household tasks, perhaps because women are supposed to do everything at home and never to ask for help.

In your job search, your first and most important resource is your friends. They are the other members of the team you've always been on, even though you've never noticed. They will refer you to other people who will refer you to other people who may have the job you're looking for. If you can't call up Rose's husband, Charles, at his office and tell him "I'm exploring the job market and although I have no reason to believe you have a job, or even know about one, I'd like to talk to you about some of the actions I'm considering," you will have to rethink your goals and perhaps decide to brush up on your shorthand. It is unlikely you will find a management job without the aid of your friends and their friends.

Friends are there to support and appreciate you, give you cups of coffee and lend you combs and lipsticks. *Talk to your friends.* Conversations with friends are characterized by mutual evaluation support, interest in your concerns. If you wish, you can organize yourselves into weekly or bi-weekly meetings to discuss the job market if several of you are looking. (It oughtn't to be a secret.) Trading information and feelings is important to you, especially at this vulnerable time. Friends are important, particularly at those times you think the tunnel is too long and somebody has boarded up the opening at the other end, anyway. Friends love each other. When somebody loves you, you feel important. You need that feeling when you're out there pounding the pavements. (See also Chapter 4, *Your Marketing Plan, Personal Contacts.*)

The Library

Don't be afraid to ask your friends for favors and don't harbor prejudices about the usefulness of your local public library. You will find it an invaluable source of information.

In the Business Reference section there are hundreds of volumes and directories giving all kinds of information about businesses, ranging from banks to public interest groups and nonprofit organizations to advertising agencies and retail stores. Listings give the names of the important executives, the products and services of every company, annual sales volumes, locations of offices and factories, even the names and locations of competitors. Trade publications and trade associations often have placement sections and one can contact appropriate people within these groups.

Use *Standard Rate and Data* when you want to look up the publications read by people in specific fields. It is a large soft-cover volume giving the names of all the trade publications in every imaginable category. It includes the names of publishers and editors and addresses and telephone numbers. A large part of it is devoted to information about advertising rates and circulation, but you don't care about that, so ignore it.

The reference librarian is expert in locating information for you . . . that's what she is paid and trained to do, so if you have a question or are confused, ask for assistance.

Depending on the size of your local library, probably it will have a section devoted to *Careers* (331.Ref in the Dewey Decimal System). There will be in this section any number of books and pamphlets about jobs and job hunts and how to write a resumé or behave at interviews, what to say to the receptionist, etc. Don't bother with most of that stuff. Right now you are interested in two major reference works. The first, published by the United States Department of Labor, is a vast and comprehensive tome entitled the *Dictionary of Occupational Titles* (the DOT). Don't be intimidated by its size. It contains the name and definition of every job known to the Department of Labor, from the lowliest hourly wage earner to definitions of the duties and responsibilities of officers of giant industrial corporations. The bulk of the information concerns jobs you don't care about, so don't worry about the remarkable size of the book. You're not going to have to read it from cover to cover and nobody is going to give you a test.

You want to study it in order to determine the names of positions suitable for someone with your particular background and interests. You have in hand your *ideal job description* so you are able to define the actions you want to take in the position you accept. Armed with the further knowledge the DOT gives you, you will be competent to tell interviewers what your career goals are and you will know which departments within a company hold within them opportunities to perform the kinds of actions you have decided you want to perform. This will give you the ability to zero in on your special target, the job with your name.

There are nine occupational categories in the DOT, each with an identifying index code number. All occupations and titles are number coded, so as you narrow your search to a particular occupation, you will be using a logical series of expanding code numbers precisely targeting your occupational goal. The addition of each digit narrows the field and gets you closer to your particular job. Basic occupational categories are as follows:

0/1 Professional, Technical and Managerial Occupations

2 Clerical and Sales Occupations

3 Service Occupations

4 Agricultural, Fishery, Forestry, and Related Occupations

5 Processing Occupations

6 Machine Trades Occupations

7 Benchwork Occupations

8 Structural Work Occupations

9 Miscellaneous Occupations

Within each of these broad categories are occupational divisions which break down the various occupational possibilities still further, adding additional digits to the identifying codes with each breakdown. For example, in order to find a category using the word *administration,* as well as an area which deals with verbal and interpersonal skills, look under the occupational category of Professional, Technical and Managerial Occupations (0/1), and discover a two digit classification, *Occupations in Administrative Specializations* (16), and within this category is a third one, coded 165, *Public Relations Management Occupations*. This general classification is defined as including

. . . occupations concerned with selection and development of favorable persuasive material and the distribution through personal contact or various communications media, in order to promote good will, develop credibility, or create favorable public image for individual, establishment, group or organization. Includes both generalists and specialists working either as an outside consultant or in-house staff member.

Count on bureaucratic language transforming an occupation largely dependent on talk, camaraderie, persuasion and lunches into something stodgy and boring!

Further under this subheading of 165 *(Public Relations Management Occupations),* there are five additional sub-job units listed, each with its own code number and detailed job description. These jobs include *lobbyist, public relations representative, song plugger* and *sales-service promoter.*

You can see how detailed and thorough the DOT is. Whatever job is offered you, if it has a title, will be described within these pages. So it behooves you in advance of the job offer to become familiar with the various job titles and inherent responsibilities most nearly describing what you want to do.

There is much cross-referencing. The back of the book contains a huge index of all the job titles and their code numbers, as well as a comprehensive index of industries. The kind of thing in which you've discovered you are interested will be found in more than one place, so there is scant chance it will slip through the cracks.

The other work you need to familiarize yourself with is called *The Encyclopedia of Careers,* and is published by the P. G. Ferguson Publishing Co. in Chicago (a subsidiary of Doubleday). It comes in two big volumes.

This material is intended for the use of young people just starting out after finishing school. There are little notes and asides to Guidance Counselors and parents who, presumably, are interested in young people's vocational selections. Since you are selecting and starting your career too, you have that same need for illumination. Don't let your advanced age throw you. The books will be useful to you, too.

The first volume has to do with *Planning Your Career.* There is a Foreward, an Introduction, explanations of how to use the material and various inspirational articles about the rewards of working for a living. Continue onward to the classification of *Career Fields.* There is an essay, written by an appropriate expert about every conceivable business and industry, from the Advertising Business to the Intercity Bus Industry to Local and State Government Service to Truck Transportation. Each of these essays is minutely detailed, laced with carefully worded definitions, descriptions of training necessary or requirements for entry level positions, an overall view of the industry and where it fits into the national picture. If you are familiar with the industry when you are interviewed for a job within it, your interviewer will note your sophistication. Your familiarity with the business will indicate to her you care, that you are intelligent and have not been sitting around watching soap operas for the past fifteen years. She doesn't have to know your knowledge is due to a couple of recent afternoons spent in the library. The payoff is well worth the effort.

The second volume of the *Encyclopedia* is entitled *Careers and Occupations.* This information is organized in a way in which it can be used in conjunction with the nine DOT basic occupational classifications; its information is not contained in the DOT, however, but is designed to flesh out that data and to give helpful perspective when both works are used jointly. For example, using the DOT reference code, the following information is included in *The Encyclopedia of Careers* about the occupation *Buyers* (162.157): a definition of the job itself, the history of the occupation, what a *buyer* does, what you have to know in order to be one, opportunities for experience and exploration, methods of entering the field, advancement, employment outlook, earnings (this is rapidly obsolete, of course, but it gives a relative picture of where the particular occupation stands in comparison to others), conditions at work, social and psychological factors and sources of additional information (a bibliography which is pertinent to each specific occupation).

Each job category is outlined this way, using these same paragraph headings. You don't have to have the DOT at your elbow to use the *Encyclopedia.* You can read it and receive good help from it on its own. A very useful, very interesting book.

When you have finished studying these three volumes you ought to have a good idea of the possibilities out there and where you are most likely to fit, particularly when you refer regularly back to your *ideal job description.*

Conventions and Trade Associations

Trade associations have annual meetings and conventions. Look through the mammoth *Encyclopedia of Associations* at the library and discover the awesome compulsion of Americans to join together in groupings of one sort or another. If you live in a big city there will be a city convention bureau which can give you a listing of organizations planning meetings in some of the hotels and meeting centers. Talk as well with the banquet or convention managers in the hotels. Find out who is coming to town and see if you can obtain an advance program or other material from the group itself. Discover who is in charge of various aspects of the meetings, association big shots who head committees, speakers and workshop leaders. When you know the names of these people, you can write them, telephone them or visit them in person.

You want to meet people and talk to them. The more people you talk to, the better your chances are. Don't think of these encounters as job interviews; think of them as information-gathering sessions. People will talk to you and they will see you. Conventioneers are like that; they are away from home and feeling expansive. Haunt the hotel lobby, see if you can sit in on open meetings. That is an excellent way to meet people. If you are prepared to tell about yourself briefly ("I'm exploring the job market and am interested in finding out more about the meat packing industry. I'm eager to meet some of the people who know about job opportunities . . ." Or, "I'm exploring the job market . . . as Chairman of the meat packers' committee on public affairs, I'm interested in knowing about the particular problems you face, how you deal with them and where a person with my background and experience might fit in. I'd like to know, too, about *you* and how you got to be the head of this particular committee"), people will generally help you out, especially if you pick people who may not be used to fielding questions like the ones you have. People in trade associations are generally not nearly so smooth and unapproachable as are people with carpeted offices on the fortieth floor. Association people are more apt to be politicians (they're generally elected to their positions) and they are friendlier, more gregarious. You will find them easier to approach for that reason.

Use the *Reader's Guide to Periodical Literature* and newspaper indexes to locate articles written in newspapers and magazines about the subject in which you're interested (meat packing), or to find stories and mentions of the company or association or person you will visit or write or telephone.

Learn to think on your feet. This takes careful listening and concentration and as little self-consciousness as possible. If the conversation is not proving fruitful in the way you thought it would, take a new tack. Don't give up. Perhaps the person to whom you are talking has another expertise you don't know about. Ask. *You have nothing to lose.* Your friendliness, your enthusiasm and interest will shine through no matter how frightened and uncomfortable you are at first. Always remember the more people you talk to, the better the chances are somebody will say, "Hey, you should talk to Philo Vance, he's been looking for somebody like you." No one can say this to you if you aren't talking with him.

It gets easier and more fun with each encounter.

It is a good idea, if you can afford it, to have business cards printed for the people you meet at your convention hopping. Your name, address and telephone number is sufficient. Handing out your card gives you the opportunity to ask somebody else for his card. Then you're off and running. Don't worry if they come from some far-away place. If they are members of an association convening in your hometown, undoubtedly they know people who work in your city. Referrals to those people are what you're after.

Employment Agencies / Ads / Personnel Departments / Executive Recruiters

Other resources you may want to probe are employment agencies, want ads, personnel departments and executive recruiting firms.

Personnel departments rarely have anything to do with hiring people. What the personnel department does is maintain company records about company employees: benefits, compensation structures and plans, insurance programs, applications and dates of promotions, transfers, hires and fires. It is a common misconception defining the personnel department as having a major role in the selection and hiring process. Personnel serves as a record keeper. *Never* go to the personnel department unless you are applying for a job as a secretary, clerk or hourly *(nonexempt)* wage earner. Always go to your contact within the company, even if she has nothing whatever to do with the area in which you've decided you want to work. Personnel people are not usually able to hire you for a middle-management job; they can *recommend* you and they do that rarely because they hate to go out on a limb. (Remember, staff people are not risk-takers.) The manager of the department in which you're interested is the person who has the authority to hire you and the knowledge to recognize your qualifications. Personnel will deal with your papers, the forms you fill out and your status if you become an employee. Most likely they won't participate in the decision about whether the company wants you.

People who have terrific *interpersonal skills* rarely go into personnel work because it has little to do with relationships between people, which is what they want—even though one tends to assume the personnel department is the place which deals most importantly with the needs of people.

Human resources is the area you will find in a company dealing with people's careers in a more personal way. Again, the people there are not the ones who are authorized to hire you unless you are looking to work within that department.

When you're looking for a career, steer clear of *personnel* and *human resources*. It's a waste of time; they are there to weed you out.

The same may be said of classified ads in general although there are exceptions. *Blind* ads have box numbers instead of addresses and ask for you to send in your resume without knowing to whom it is going. Most likely you will be sending it to an employment agency or to a personnel department. See if you can imagine why you should send your resumé to an employment agency or to the personnel department if the advertisement is for a *manager of public affairs*, especially if a personnel department doesn't hire people. Wouldn't it make more sense if your resumé went to the public affairs department straight away? Why deal with the middle man? Because the people in the public affairs department don't want to waste their time reading resumés (public affairs is a popular field), they give this time-consuming task to the personnel department or to an agency. After a functionary there has gone through the mail he will throw out most of the replies to the ad and then send the ones left to the person in the public affairs department who will make the interviewing decisions. With your unconventional background, the personnel staffer will never take the risk of sending your resumé on to the hiring manager. Since he doesn't make the hiring decision he must serve the letter of the *job order*. If he goes outside of that outline, he might end up looking foolish and he doesn't want to do that. You can't expect the personnel manager or the employment agency to slip your resumé in with the others, it is not a useful expectation.

It makes you feel more comfortable to go through personnel channels, of course, precisely because you know there isn't any risk. The activity lulls you into thinking you're making headway. *Keep your eye on the sparrow.*

You should be talking to people who are in a position to help or hire you.

You probably stand a better chance with an employment agency than you do with a company personnel department, but the outlook is still fairly bleak. Don't look for advice at an employment agency, or from someone who cares about what happens to you. Employment agencies are paid by the company in which they place somebody and they don't get paid if some other agency comes along first with someone else who is hired. For this reason, each agency must work as fast and furiously as possible to fill vacancies and it doesn't matter to them if they are offering you your dream job or not. They want somebody hired—

fast. So they don't have much patience with you if you have any questions or if you tell them the position doesn't suit you. They lose money spending time with you.

My experience has taught me never to recommend my clients to seek help from executive recruiters. Recruiters don't know about housewives *at all.* Executive recruiters are hired on an advance fee, or "retainer," basis, which differentiates them from employment agencies which are paid only when one of their candidates is hired. Companies hire executive recruiters to locate people for specific openings, usually in the $25,000-and-up range. Unless you have an unusual background of visible management experience (heavyweight volunteer work like being in charge of Planned Parenthood for the entire state of Ohio or President of the North-Central League of Women Voters), no executive recruiter will be willing to spend any time with you unless he has some slave job in his own office.

You are not a representative of the pool of potential candidates with which he is familiar and to which he goes whenever his corporate client gives him an assignment, so don't take his rejection personally.

His stock in trade is his ability to locate top management talent in a circumscribed, narrowly defined field; he must have the ability to evaluate and to persuade: He must evaluate a candidate's potential performance and "fit" and he must be able to persuade the candidate to accept the offer when it comes, and persuade the client the particular person he has selected is the best one for the position. How could he persuade anybody of your business-world qualifications? He doesn't know himself what they are. If the recruiter is a good one, he understands his client thoroughly and knows precisely those things the client requires in the people who work for him. The people who succeed in corporate life, the people who hire recruiters and themselves are selected by recruiters, are all the same people. They are easily recognized by one another. For them it's like looking in the mirror. A woman, especially a *housewife,* is a Martian. It is nothing against the businessman, it's just that nothing in a business experience prepares him for dealing with such a person. So don't bother trying to make some executive recruiter figure out what to do with you. He might hire you himself but he will *never* recommend you to a client.

Should You Go Back to School?

Of course it may turn out you don't want a job after all. You may need something quite else, something you can't put your finger on. You may think this sense of yearning, or sense of personal worthlessness may best be assuaged by enrolling in college and earning the degree you neglected so long ago.

I did this and have never regretted it. Going back to school opened doors and enriched my outlook, my approach to myself and to life around me. Probably such eye opening couldn't have happened otherwise. I had suffered until I was thirty-five or so with an acute and dreadful sense of intellectual inferiority. The fact I did well at college and in graduate school was beneficial to me. The process of going to school, listening to lectures, learning to read with perception and skepticism, participating in rigorous discussions, evaluating material and writing papers containing my carefully considered points of view were all necessary to my growth. I could not have gone out and found an interesting job if I had not learned to trust my brain power. Certainly I would never have had the nerve to go into business for myself. College showed me I was competent.

On the other hand, many women who do not have college degrees already feel intelligent and comfortable with their intellectual capacities. Such people may have other reasons for wanting to go to college. They may need advanced degrees for professional vocations. They may think you must have a baccalaureate in order to obtain a decent job, especially in the competitive job marketplace of today. That's probably correct for young people because a college degree represents today what a high school diploma meant when I was twenty-one. However, a mature woman already has sufficient *life experience* and it is transferrable to a business-world setting, unlike the still-green twenty-one-year-old college graduates who have no such comparable experience, despite their new credentials. Most jobs don't require technical or professional training anyhow. The reentering woman doesn't have to have a degree if she can point to hard experience as a volunteer or part-time worker, or can demonstrate her qualifications and capacity in some other appropriate way.

Going back to college can get you into gear, can rev your motor and blow away the cobwebs. It is a stimulating process and if you can afford expenditures of the money and time, and if you think you will profit from the experience, by all means do so.

If you go back to school in order to delay your attempt to enter the world of paid workers, that is not a good reason. In that case college enrollment may be a device you invent in order to prevent the necessity of facing the music and deciding what to do with yourself once the children are grown. You should know it if that's what you're doing.

Careful introspection is what is called for and it comes down, once again, to your private reflection on what is best for you.

In Summary

So far you've been doing a lot of introspection and library work and writing down and musing on the nature of your interests and personal style and the likely whereabouts of the place in the world of work where you will be looking. You've been concerned with the resources available to you and have learned your intelligence, your tenacity and imagination, your commitment are your "bottom line" resources. You are going to find your job yourself. You will seek and receive help all along the way, but the effort and the rewards will be yours alone. You understand and accept reality: No job will fall from heaven. The person you heard about who received a fabulous job offer from a stranger standing next to her at the bus stop is as likely as is your being picked to appear on "Let's Make a Deal" in your shredded coconut outfit. The friend I have who wanted me to find him an "agent" because he had "lots of ideas for movies" will never write a movie script any more than the girl who spends her time drinking sodas at the drug store in Hollywood will become a movie star. Ideas are cheap. Making dreams come true requires planning, organization, discipline and action.

When you admit to yourself there are no such things as little pink elves and fairies dancing under mushrooms, then you take responsibility for your fate and begin to understand you can make it happen yourself by taking practical action. That's good news. You will select your *modus operandi*. You will throw overboard the silly advice or the conventional job search techniques which in your case are unworkable. When somebody says, "Oh, a resumé should *never* be more than one page," you will ask yourself *why not?*

You may be getting impatient, a good sign. People who are eager to begin a job search are motivated to get past those first ugly bumps. Now is a good time to notice what you have already done:

1. Decided to look for a job.
2. Determined what you will be happiest doing.
3. Written your *ideal job description*.
4. Spent some time at the library matching up the possibilities in the world of work with your ambitions and qualifications.

None of these actions has been performed in a vacuum. All along, simultaneous with the prescribed tasks, you've been thinking, assessing, sorting out, making decisions. You read the *Industries* section of the *Encyclopedia of Careers* with your own vicinity in mind; you are aware of the possibilities and the limitations of its geography, and what businesses are located within it. Other considerations having to do with the constraints of family life have occurred to you as well.

You have probably spent three weeks in this process, which is about average. If you take too much longer than that, you can begin to wonder how serious you are. Too much quicker and you can wonder the same thing. Again, however, everyone has her private sets of priorities. If it feels right, probably it is right.

You are almost ready to go out and start talking to

people. Here are the rest of your tasks, which will be accomplished in short order:

1. Writing your resumé.
2. Organizing your job campaign.
3. Obtaining interviews.
4. Participating in interviews.
5. Assessing the possibilities.
6. Accepting the job offer.

The entire campaign will probably take six months. That may sound creakingly slow. It isn't. Even if you are careful and thoughtful, you may still run up against catastrophes or surprises. A goal of six months is reasonable because it is a period of time in which a number of unforeseen events can be integrated without loss of important enthusiasm and energy. It holds within it permission for you to get bogged down and depressed and to recover and continue.

Remember your pregnancies and how fast the first six months went by? Remember what you were doing six months *ago?* Time flies. Six months turns out to be short indeed when you're looking for a job and planning what you're going to be doing for a good part of the rest of your life.

CHAPTER THREE

The Resumé

A JOB SEARCH IS A SALES CAMPAIGN, SO IT IS A FINE idea to examine the process with the same kind of impersonal scrutiny a sales manager uses when he looks over his objectives. When something goes haywire in a carefully constructed sales campaign, the sales manager stands back and figures out which component needs attention. He is interested in results, and so are you. You too have to detach yourself from the personal and emotional aspects of your job search in order to make it work.

Basically, a sales campaign is made up of five components:

1. The product
2. The market
3. The promotional material
4. The sales presentation
5. The purchase

In your job campaign:

1. *You* are the *product*.
2. The *market* consists of *potential employers*.
3. The *promotional brochure* is your *resumé*.

4. *Interviews* are your *sales presentations*.
5. The *purchase* is made when you receive a *job offer*.

In this chapter we are concerned with the promotional material for your sales campaign: your resumé.

The Purpose of Your Resumé

Probably nothing else in the entire job search process holds within it possibilities for so many misconceptions as does the resumé and its preparation. For some reason, people feel very strongly about resumés: how they should look, what they should say, how important (or unimportant) they are to the overall scheme of things.

Since it is your resumé, you must decide the best way to design and use it.

While you may believe the purpose of your resumé is to get you a job offer, it isn't. Its purpose is *to favorably impress the person who reads it*. This positive reaction takes you one step closer to achieving the goal of a job offer. Your resumé does not stand alone. It is part of the tapestry of the whole job campaign: It fits in with the other threads just as the self-evaluation produces your *ideal job description* and the techniques you use to obtain interviews.

The formula you use when writing your resumé is the same one you use when designing the job campaign's other components:

$$\text{Purpose (Style + Substance)} = \frac{\text{Positive Reaction of}}{\text{Potential Employer}}$$

The body of the resumé may change slightly in relationship to the way it is used; it will never change much. It is unwise to tailor a resumé to a specific job. The purpose of your resumé is *not* reactive. Its purpose is to *cause* a reaction. This can best be accomplished when you give your strengths first priority by emphasizing them honestly and clearly. If you were to write a resumé for every job you heard about, you would never do anything but write resumés. Because it is a description of the experience you've had up to now which is transferrable to business, the story on your resumé will not change much unless you discover new things about yourself.

Number of Pages

People who get prickly when you show them a two- or three-page resumé often tell you "no one will read more than one page. . . . They read hundreds of resumés every day. . . . Their eyes are tired. . . . They will hate you for making them work so hard. . . . They will throw away your resumé to punish you. . . . Only conceited people or hopelessly ignorant ones produce resumés of more than one page. . . ."

These people don't know what they're talking about. Reflect for a moment. Who reads hundreds of resumés every day? The Director of Public Relations? Is that his job? The Bookkeeping Manager? The Chief of Manufacturing? Of course not. Secretaries in the personnel department whose job it is to open the mail read hundreds of resumés every month as they weed them out and file them away. Personnel department people who are in charge of hiring clerks and secretaries and keeping records of potential clerks and secretaries read resumés every day. People in middle-management positions do *not* read hundreds of resumés every day because they are not paid to do that particular chore. When they have a job opening someone else is charged with the task of screening the resumés. The hiring manager will be presented with a small, carefully selected pile of resumés—if he gets any at all—but he will not have read anything like a hundred resumés by the time he hires someone and he will certainly not concern himself with unsolicited resumés. He is busy directing public relations every day—not reading resumés.

As your resumé will be read by a hiring manager later, not earlier in your relationship with him, you want to present yourself so he will react favorably. He cannot do that if your story is too short for him to make a competent judgment about your quality or possible value to his department.

* * *

Substance

Whatever format you select for your resumé, whatever style you decide to use, it must communicate your overall ability and the specific experience which demonstrates this ability. The way people determine the likelihood of excellence in future performance is when they see whether past performance was characterized by excellence. Every smart employer wants excellence in his employees, because he knows such excellence makes him look good and helps "the bottom line." So it is excellence in what you have done, not previous job titles, you want to convey in a resumé.

Your promotional document must be succinct and persuasive, must sound businesslike and must be used in a businesslike way.

The body of a resumé is divided into several categories. You can put them in the sequence which you feel tells your story most cogently. The categories, and the conventional order for them, are:

1. Your objective
2. Your education
3. Your experience
4. Additional information such as your honors, awards, memberships, associations, clubs, hobbies, etc.

1. Objective. The purpose of the short *objective* category in your resumé is to demonstrate your understanding of your skills and interests and to suggest how they can be transferred to a business setting. It does not dictate a specific position or title. While you cannot predict accurately where you are going to end up, you can predict what you will be doing in a general way because you know what you like to do and what you're good at. The objective should be brief and to the point, no more than two sentences. Use action verbs and steer clear of adjectives and adverbs, so the sentences will be not only vivid and interesting, but energetic, too, definitely characteristics you want to emphasize to a potential employer.

Here is a sample *objective:*

* * *

My career objective will use my organizational and communications skills. I will collect and analyze data, interact with colleagues, transmit information in written reports.

Another:

My career objective is a position in which I will use my communications skills. I will explain programs and policies through written and oral means.

Or:

My career objective is a position in which I will use my motivational and communications skills. I will persuade people to a specific point of view or action through use of the techniques I have developed as a public speaker and educator.

As you can see, the *objective* has been cribbed from your *ideal job description*.

The *objective* must be a logical outgrowth of your ambition and your aptitude (interests). Keep it broad enough to encompass more than one possibility. You can describe what a salesman does without saying you want to be a salesman. Many positions other than straight sales jobs use the same skills of persuasion and motivation. The moment you say your objective is a job in the sales department, you are closing off other options. The reader of your resumé will not have the imagination to figure out where else your skills might fit you. So don't narrow the field until the last possible moment.

When people read something, they tend to accept the words they read more completely and unquestioningly than they would if the words were spoken. The written word adds power and legitimacy to any idea, even a crackpot one. So choose carefully what you say on your resumé. Don't put anything in your *objective* you don't understand or don't believe. As a matter of fact, the *objective*, since it must be simply and clearly stated, is probably the hardest sentence to write in the entire resumé. You may want to leave the writing of it until last. (I think it was Mark Twain who wrote a friend saying "I apologize for the length of this letter but I don't have time to write a short one.")

Use the methods you used when you were designing your *ideal job*. Think of the actions which please you and translate these actions into words which seem appropriate when talking about what happens in the business world.

Everything in a resumé is of a piece. Once you've determined your product (what you are selling to your prospective employer), then every sentence in your product brochure must either explain, enlarge upon, demonstrate, or suggest uses for the product. The resumé's *objective* suggests the *use* for your product.

2. Education. If you graduated from college, this information should be included, along with your course of study, right up front, with the date of your graduation, even if it was in 1913. Don't presume if you omit the date no one will notice its omission. Everyone will notice it, it will stick out like an *x* in a row of *o*'s and you will be put on the defensive the moment the subject comes up. One of the advantages about you is you weren't born yesterday. Remember you are not entering a beauty contest. You are looking to enter the job force at a middle-management level. Competence, intelligence, clearheadedness are the characteristics you are selling and youth is not a requirement, or even a component of these qualifications. In fact, youth quite often operates against them. For once, you can set aside the tiresome obligation imposed on women (and accepted by them, worse to say) having to do with the presumption youth is better. Undoubtedly people will tell you, if you are over the age of forty, that your age is a tremendous handicap in the job market. Don't believe it, don't put on layers of makeup and dye your hair. You are who you are and your acceptance of and confidence in yourself will be what is most convincing in your presentation. Since you can't do anything about how old you are, you might as well make it a plus.

It is. Good judgment is more often a characteristic of someone over forty than someone under forty.

If you attended college but didn't graduate, include the name of the institution and the years you attended. If you were there for more than a year, you can include a couple of the courses you took. That will serve to indicate a seriousness of academic purpose, even if it was interrupted or concluded at that time.

List any additional courses you've taken over the years, including graduate work. If you have a graduate degree, that should go first on the list, even if it is in a discipline which you no longer want to pursue. Always start with the most recently completed degree. Additional courses independent of degree work should be included last. You don't have to list everything you've ever taken (omit the Contract Bridge Class at the Adult School). Select each item to enhance the overall picture.

3. *Experience.* Most resumés make an orderly list of jobs, years held and titles, starting with the most recent first. The assumption is, in most cases, since the title of the job tells its story, the reader doesn't need much additional explanation because the recital will be redundant, take up space, and bore the reader. This is wrongheaded. Job titles by themselves very often *confuse* the reader. There should always be a brief explanation of what you did, no matter how clearly you think the title defines the position. The most effective skill the president of a company has may be salesmanship; another president might be terrible at sales but terrific at financial planning and numbers. You can see titles don't tell nearly enough.

Quite often resumés get bogged down in silly ways. For some reason, people who make their livings writing resumés for other people (professional resumé-writing services can be found in the yellow pages of every major city) are terrified of using the first person pronoun, even if the form of the verb calls for it:

Responsible for preparing and distributing payroll every week.

Was in charge of calling on customers.

What's the matter with saying "I"? Using the appropriate pronoun doesn't make you sound conceited. It is the way English is properly written.

Avoid use of the passive voice. In the passive voice, things happen *to* you instead of you making them happen. The verbs you select and the way you use them demonstrate your vigor and your ability to take charge. Say "my responsibilities include . . ." or "As supervisor of the seven-member telephone pool, my charter included . . ." and then follow with energetic verbs.

In order to discover the things about yourself you want to sell, you will have to examine your experience closely. You may or may not want to include the paid jobs you've had. They may be irrelevant. For example, when I started looking for a paid job in 1976, the last full-time employment I'd had was as a pencil sharpener and mail deliverer office girl at Time Inc., nineteen years before, in 1957. That's a classy place to have worked, but nothing else about the data is impressive. I dazzled people for years when I told them I had worked at *Life* magazine (I rarely disclosed my duties) but in a resumé you have to tell what you did in order to show you are qualified to do important, effective work elsewhere using the same skills. Since I no longer wanted to be an office girl and the skills I had developed as an office girl were not the ones I wanted to use in the future, I had to throw out the information as useless.

As a writer of your resumé, you may learn the red pencil is as important to you as is a clean sheet of paper.

In order to learn what your experience is, you will have to undertake a list-writing assignment. As far as I've been able to determine, there is no other way to get at this information. It's all there, in your hand, but you have to dig to get it all out so you can select the most significant aspects of it.

What you must do is make a list of at least fifteen things you are proud of having done in your life. They don't necessarily have to relate to paid work. They can come from any time in your life. It might occur to you to include running a bake sale for your church, knitting a ski sweater despite the impossible-to-understand instructions. The point of the list is to ennumerate your accomplishments. Don't make the list right away. Take a couple of days and then sit down and write it. You will find you will include things you haven't thought about for years (the two days wait will give your mysterious subconscious a chance to ferret out and push forward the important but forgotten activities). Read over the list but don't censor it or leave things off because they're not important or because they sound boring or idiotic. Nobody is going to see the list except you.

If you have more than fifteen achievements on your list that's terrific. Keep writing as long as you feel like it. If you can't think of fifteen accomplishments, think some more. And be a little curious about why you can't think of anything you take pride in having done. Are your expectations too high? Do you value too little the actions you have taken in your life, or the contributions you've made? How's your self-esteem? Could you use an injection of self-confidence?

Check for passive voice accomplishments: "Being selected as one out of one hundred twenty-five other students to represent my sorority at a national Pan-Hellenic conference." That recognition didn't fall upon you as the gentle rain from heaven. You must have done some politicking. Think back, remember. The way you express yourself, the way you describe what you do reveals your opinion of yourself. Change the passive voice to active and demonstrate your ability to make a positive impact on your environment.

Now you have this list of achievements you know what you consider your major accomplishments. You reached each of your goals through a series of actions you planned and implemented.

You imposed your unique viewpoint on each accomplishment and you acted in a particular style in order to achieve it.

Next, pick your five favorite achievements on the list. For each, write one or two paragraphs explaining what your original objective was (the problem or situation you wanted resolved through your action), what action steps enabled you to reach that objective, and what the result of your actions was. Sometimes the result is different and better than the original intention, so you want to differentiate the result from the objective. If the result outshines the objective, examination of the action steps you took will probably disclose the reason you achieved something even more significant to you than you had planned.

The sequence of ideas you will use when you write these paragraphs is as follows:

Objective (Problem): Action Steps: Result

Sue H., long a stalwart volunteer in local community politics (her village had a population of 7,500 people), felt her efforts were not necessarily valuable or transferrable since she had never worked on a successful campaign and the one time she herself had run for office, she had been defeated.

"Who wants a loser?" she shrugged.

Despite this attitude about the episode, this item was included on her list of achievements: "Ran for Town Council and received the support of both warring factions in our badly fragmented party organization."

"How did you accomplish this?" I asked.

It turned out that keeping both factions calm and working for her had been no easy task. It had required large doses of diplomacy, skillful negotiation and courage. She was too modest to admit any of these things and didn't feel comfortable bragging. She felt much more comfortable giving the credit to others. She had to face, however, what distinct contribution she had made. I told her to omit all adjectives and describe how she had accomplished her goal.

In order to win the respect of both sides without needlessly compromising her position and in order to gain the help she needed (her objective), she had decided she had to be rigorous about her views, back up her opinions with solid documentation, open herself to the complaints and/or advice of both sides. It was a mini-campaign within the larger one and required at least as much energy and commitment. Keeping on her toes in this way probably improved her ability to deal with the public.

After we talked about that aspect of her nonelection, she seemed pleased. "Yes, keeping both sides happy *was* an accomplishment and telling about it isn't bragging when I talk about what I actually did and don't exaggerate."

The paragraphs which described her campaign activities finally looked like this:

As a candidate for local office, I had to keep both factions of my political party satisfied with me and my campaign so they would assist me. To achieve this, it was necessary to establish a communications apparatus which enabled me to maintain close, active contact with members of both factions, to disseminate information about my positions on issues and to respond quickly and firmly when problems arose. This required my thorough understanding of the issues as well as an ability to explain my positions in a persuasive, well-documented manner. In turn, this helped me in the general election. Although I lost (the district was registered 3 to 1 in favor of the opposition party), I led our local ticket.

The objective she had originally ascribed to the effort ("getting elected to public office") was not the result of her actions. As it turned out, the result was probably more significant than had been her original intention. Barring a miracle—an unlikely political event—there is very little you can do to change things around when the registration is three to one against you. Her objective had been unrealistic. The action steps she took (communicating, establishing, explaining, understanding, analyzing, persuading, documenting) revealed a skillful ability to deal with what could have been a bad experience. The paragraphs, as you can see, merely take the action steps and put them into sentence form. That's not hard to do, once you get the hang of it. It is understated, also—which is how you want your paragraphs to look and sound. There are few adjectives, no passive voice, no hidden "poor me's."

Here is another summary, written by a woman who had done only volunteer work since leaving college several years before; she had not had a paying job since before her marriage:

As a general volunteer at a well-known municipal art museum, my responsibilities ranged from selling books and materials in the book store, to explaining the advantages of membership to museum visitors at the front door during membership campaigns, to helping maintain the bookstore inventory, to operating the Museum switchboard, to acting as Admitting Receptionist.

In all of these duties I maintained familiarity with Museum policy, personnel and with permanent and special collections and events. An ability to keep a cool head under pressure was important, especially in the peak tourist seasons when Museum visitors required immediate attention and assistance.

On her list of achievements this woman had included the following interesting bit: "Calmed the ruffled feathers of a self-important foreign visitor when it was discovered there was no special tour for him as he had assumed. This was made even more difficult when it was discovered he spoke almost no English."

See how she enlarged upon this original sentence by shortening it so her ability to "keep a cool head under pressure" became the personal style she imposed on *all* her actions? An ability to stay calm and avoid panic in yourself and others is important at work. A potential employer should know this about her. She can tell the specific story of how she managed in this particular incident at the interview.

And what of the woman with the cable-knit sweater with impossible-to-follow instructions?

Using graph paper and a red grease pencil, I marked the paper precisely as the instructions called for before I started knitting the sweater. When I analyzed the diagram I had created, I discovered the instructions were wrong in one crucial area. I was able to correct this error on my diagram before I started. In this way, I became familiar with the complicated design and tackled the knitting itself with determination and confidence. Attention to detail, understanding of the overall design concept and the way to achieve it produced the first flawless cable sweater I ever knit; I received many compliments and requests for more. I feel competent now to make my own designs. I know I could write instructions which would be easy for others to follow.

She is talking about a homely task, certainly, yet she reveals herself as a tenacious, careful, goal-oriented person who is definitely not a quitter.

You may have figured out each of these paragraphs can be transferred whole quite easily to the *experience* category of your resumé. You have written five such paragraphs; pick your three favorites and use them. If you love them all, use them all. Write others and use them. Crucial experience is that which is accomplished because of your personal style. It might be something millions of other people do every day; that's not important. What is important to a potential employer is how your unique personal style has enabled you to accomplish the goals you've set for yourself.

Only you can recognize and describe what makes an episode in your life unique and why you regard it as an accomplishment.

Remember the formula:

Objective: Action Steps: Result

On occasion, I've stumbled across women who are so stubborn and unyielding they refuse to admit they know how to do anything. They cling to their supposed ineptness as if it were something to be proud of. If that's the case with you, I suggest you read the following resumé, which may give you heart. It is one I worked up with one of those women who believed her brains had turned to mud and she had nothing whatever to offer the world. She was cowed and afraid. This resumé, with minor modifications, can apply to every career housewife in the land.

It describes major transferable accomplishments.

Ruth Sloan
70 Indian Road
Columbus, Ohio 73899
(423) 385-3883

My objective is to find an interesting position which will stretch and enhance the motivational and organizational skills I have developed in my wide-ranging and unusual background.

Experience

I recently completed twenty years of experience as a suburban housewife and mother of two children.

General Management responsibilities included development and implementation of short- and long-range strategies and programs, including:

Budgeting: I was accountable for the allocation and disbursement of an annual budget averaging $25K.

Purchasing: Planned expenditures ranged from low-ticket items to heavy capital equipment and services: sound systems, major appliances, musical instruments, automobiles, carpets, furniture, medical, dental and orthodontic services, club memberships, recreational devices, travel arrangements (tours and vacations), clothes and food.

Analyzing needs and supervising the use of all material and services.

Scheduling: Set priorities, met deadlines, often directed and accomplished several important tasks at once.

Recruiting, interviewing, evaluating, selecting and assigning personnel: Persons hired and supervised included domestic workers, gardeners, painters, roofers, plumbers, handymen, electricians, carpenters, decorators, babysitters.

Persuading and Motivating: Formulated marketing strategies and sold the idea of personal development and goals definition in the form of participation in music lessons, swimming, tennis, soccer and ballet lessons, cultural events, the proper and regular use of libraries and the reading of books, visits to museums, galleries and to the movies.

Acculturating, teaching: For the two people whose care and appropriate development were under my tutelage and direction, I stood ready to respond to stated needs on a twenty-four-hour basis. I evaluated when no action was appropriate, even when requested, and took action where indicated.

<u>Selection, Design, Preparation and Provision of the following services</u>: All meals, transportation, clothing (including scheduling and supervision in order to provide clothes on a regular basis), medical service and education.

I was solely responsible for the Quality of Life in a specific place and over a period of twenty years.

A housewife is an outstanding example of what is meant by the term "a self-starter." At no time does she receive a salary for her services or for the projects in which she involves herself; she is always on call and held responsible when services break down.

Few executives have to dust the desk before they sit down to work at it. That's a perception to which executives must be educated so they can understand the importance and nearly unlimited nature of the housewife's scope and function.

4. *Hobbies or Diversions.* The reason for the inclusion of these aspects of your personality is to round out the picture for the reader of the resumé. If you like to garden, include it. An amateur gardener is a specific sort of person, a "shirt-sleeve" type, a person who is *goal-oriented*, not afraid of dirty hands, someone who likes to see tangible results from her efforts. If what you like to do in your spare time is to read, or to ski, or to jog, or to play the piano, or to listen to records, say so. Mention the two or three most important of these favorite diversions. Flesh out the picture you've painted. Give yourself extra dimension, additional interest and reality.

If you belong to any formal group or clubs, you may want to mention them here, if your membership enhances the portrait you're painting. Select carefully; don't include more than three or four memberships. You don't want to stereotype yourself as a frivolous joiner or lady bountiful in the flowered hat and silly shoes. Serious organizations are called for. If you've been active in your local political party, mention it, but remember the person who reads the information may be of a different political persuasion. Don't offend him in advance by naming which party you like best. He can ask you if he cares and then by all means be candid. It's not recommended to include any information likely to have a negative impact on the reader. The same goes for comments like "I'm a born-again Christian" or "I live by the Ten Commandments." These statements may represent laudable principles, but they have no place on a resumé.

If you've chaired or served on any committees, name them (perhaps they've been mentioned in the body of your resumé).

If you've received honors or awards from organizations or from your community, list them. Don't hide your light under a bushel; this is not the place for that.

By the way, when you're writing you should have a dictionary and a copy of *Roget's Thesaurus* close at hand. You will be amazed at how swiftly your vocabulary increases in size and strength.

Examples

It is probably a good idea here to include a couple of examples of thoughtful, carefully prepared resumés. You can't copy them, of course, but you can examine them to see how you can design and improve your resumé.

Kathryn Stewart
2841 Washington Blvd.
Indianapolis, Indiana 88336

(914) 389-0988

Objective: A position in a field where my training in English History and Language will be appropriate and important, requiring use of my motivational, organizational and administrative skills.

Education

M. Phil., Indiana University, English History, 1978.

M.A., Indiana University, English History, 1970.

B.A., Purdue University, English, 1959.

Qualifications and Experience

In the performance of organizational and administrative projects in academic and social environments, my responsibilities have included:

- Collection and analysis of data.
- Organization of information for access and retrieval.
- Research and selection of pertinent material, development of an original point of view, preparation and documentation of supporting data.
- Writing and editing original material within perimeters dictated by the requirements of scholarship and the meeting of deadlines.
- Development of reading knowledge in French and Italian.
- Creation and direction of varied projects for a group of twenty-two twelve- and thirteen-year-old Girl Scouts, including hiking, camping, sewing, cooking, teaching of parliamentary procedures and the orderly and logical running of meetings. It was necessary to plan each of these meetings carefully and in advance so that events would move along swiftly and efficiently, would hold the interest of participants and encourage them to act responsibly.
- Organization of this group of Girl Scouts into a direct sales organization for the purpose of selling over 300,000 cookies (a record for the county) in a two-month period of time. I supervised the record-keeping apparatus, the col-

lection of money, balanced the books and saw to it that all orders were promptly delivered and receivables were collected and accounted for.

Page 2   Kathryn Stewart

Other Experience

During my undergraduate training, I lived in France with a French family and went to school at the Sorbonne in Paris. Earlier, I was responsible for the purchase, preparation and distribution of all the meals for thirty students during a bike trip through southern Indiana.

In 1965, I hosted a French group of engineers who visited Pace University, in Westchester County. I arranged for a tour of the County's places of interest—including the Kensico and Croton Dams and water systems—and became expert myself to the extent I could answer questions about the city and county water supply and its history. Later, I organized a dinner party in my home for the group.

Hobbies and Memberships

Hobbies include reading, writing letters, collaborating on a cookbook to be distributed for the benefit of the Blythedale Children's Home.

I am a member of the Westchester League of Women Voters and the Scarsdale Feed-a-Waif Program.

This woman (her name has been changed) had walked into my office and wailed about her lack of purpose. "It has taken me eight years not to get a Ph.D.!" she confessed. Reflection and analysis led her to understand her important accomplishments. The first five "bulleted" items on the resumé talk about achievements at graduate school. In addition, running a troop of prepubescent girls may be

outside of the business world, but requires businesslike
skill and disciplined actions.

Emily Bellman
2388 Riverside Drive
New York, New York 10024

(212) 387-3055

Objective: A position which will demand social
commitment and the creative imposition of my
skills as an organizer and program developer.

Education

Bard College, Annondale-on-Hudson, New York,
1970.

Experience

Community Council of   Citizen Monitor
Greater New York
January 1978 to May 1979

My charter was to evaluate the effectiveness and
efficiency of the New York City YCCIP (Youth Community Conservation and Improvement Projects) and
YETP (Youth Employment and Training Programs),
both CETA funded projects.

I made formal and informal visits to the program
offices and work sites to interview project leaders, their assistants and the participants,
both in groups and individually. Since it was necessary to collect honest, uncensored information—
particularly from program recipients—I often
joined and worked along with the job teams, talking
with their members as we performed the tasks. At the
conclusion of this evaluation process, I drafted a
recommendation which included a summary of the
objective of each program, an analysis of its

leadership and activities, and a rating of its overall effectiveness and efficient use of funding.

Approximately twenty programs were thus evaluated in a fifteen-month period.

New York City 92nd Street YM-YWHA   Teacher
September 1977 to present

As a teacher of learning-disabled children, I design and initiate projects to help them learn to value themselves and their capabilities. The task requires not only sensitivity to the children's limitatons, but to their considerable talent and ingenuity as well. Objectives include improved social interaction, increased attention spans, physical dexterity and the ability to initiate and follow through on tasks. These goals are achieved through guidance, direction and encouragement of the children's participation in pantomime games, group discussions, clay modeling, weaving, cutting, drawing, painting, etc.

The National Crafts Council   Researcher
March 1973 to February 1974

I organized and administered all lending, shipping and returns for slide kit orders, handled all of this department's correspondence, including correspondence with artists and craftsmen who had ideas for potential slide kits or wanted to know the status of kits in progress. Interaction, both oral and written, with the general public was required, necessitating thorough knowledge of nation-wide craft events and opportunities as well as educational facilities.

As an integral part of my work I established rapport with craftsmen and learned to deal with their problems and expectations with tact and understanding.

The Women's National Abortion Office Manager and
Action Coalition   Public Relations
                                     Manager

September 1972 to February 1973

For this national political organization which focused on an extremely controversial and sensitive issue, I created layouts for advertising, wrote copy for pamphlets and ads for national distribution. I prepared layouts and mechanicals for the monthly newspaper, met deadlines, dealt with graphics people and printers. I worked closely with representatives of other organizations, such as Planned Parenthood, NARAL, etc.

I was the Coalition representative at various conferences; I researched, prepared and delivered speeches and participated in debates.

I organized celebrity fund-raising events, including supervising site selection and arrangements, accommodating visiting dignitaries, and generally keeping things perking along and running smoothly.

I was also in charge of interviewing persons who had had illegal abortions. From these often emotion-charged interviews I extrapolated pertinent data and prepared it for presentation in writing and in person at the New York State abortion hearings. I organized, interviewed and supervised several volunteers who worked with me on the project.

References available on request.

It should be noted all of Ms. Bellman's experience is volunteer. At no time was she paid wages for any of the things she accomplished. Yet she held responsibilities of vital importance to the organizations she represented.

What Not to Do

In case you're tempted to envy men as the repositories of all business knowledge, let me assure you it isn't the case. Men have been operating in business situations on a much larger scale and in greater numbers and for a longer period of time than have women. They are far more accustomed to the jargon and the way it is At The Office than are we. However, there are just as many dumb men out there as dumb women in here.

This seems like a good time to include a resumé of a man who has worked for pay since he got out of school—and has been successful at it, judging from the cut of his jacket and the expensive nature of his carefully blown-dry hairdo. This is a legitimate document, given to me in 1979, in all earnestness by the person whose resumé it is, who seemed to be complimented when I asked him if I could keep a copy. Only the names have been changed to protect the innocent.

Joseph W. Whitmore
293 Buena Vista Avenue
Los Angeles, California 38478

Personal

Divorced, one child	Height	-5'10"
Health, Excellent	Weight	-165 pounds
Hobbies, Tennis,		
Riding, Reading	Birth	-21 February 1931

Education

Stamford University, A.B. degree with Honors, 1952
Zurich School of Economics, Graduate Studies in Economics, 1953
Chicago University Graduate School of Business, 1957–1959
University of California at Davis Graduate School of Business, 1963–1964

Business Experience

Merwyn Development Corporation, New York City
Industrial and Commercial Real Estate
1971–Present, Vice President, Development

New York City Municipal Transfer Corporation
   1970–1972
      Vice President, Finance, Administration and
      Facilities

BEKCA MANINC, Los Angeles, California
   1967–1970
      Management Consultants—Founder and President

Sunray Industries, Beverly Hills, California
   1966–1967
   Advanced Naval Technology Division—Fast Deploy-
ment Logistic Ship Project—Senior Program Administrator
      1960–1964
         Member of Executive Staff—Sunray Systems, Inc.
            Manager of Administration, Systems
            Laboratory
            Manager of Administration, Computer
            Production

Branch Aircraft Company, KP-2 Program Office
   1965–1966
      Project Coordinator

Bonick Products Group—the commercial activity of
Bonick Industries, Los Angeles
   1959–1960
      Management Planner—Member of Planning and
         Operations
      Analysis Staff for Group Vice President and
General Manager

Nystrio Corporation, Inc., New York City
   Assistant to the President until 1959

Tiedke's Department Store, New York City
   Executive Training Program, 1954

Other Activities

I have served on the Board of Directors of several
companies and have been active in political campaigns on both a state and local level.

He got the whole thing on one page and I wonder what

good it did. It looks cramped and unprofessional. In fact the format actually works against ease in reading.

What hits you first about the information he has decided to include? You can't miss what he feels is most important about himself.

Divorced, one child.

I have used this resumé as a basis for discussion in several workshops and the reactions are always the same: "Why does he put the news of his divorce *first?*" "Is *that* the most important information about him?"

Placement of information on your sales brochure has much to do with the effect you want.

Since people who read this resumé react strongly, instantly and negatively to the piece of information which he has decided to put first, its position in the document is incorrect. If marital status has a place in a resumé (I don't believe it does unless it is a housewife's resumé, in which case the information will explain her absence from the paid work force and should be included with the ages and number of her children at the end) it belongs someplace other than the first sentence.

The placement of *hobbies* is peculiar, too. Why should this news comes before the *experience* section? Does this imply the writer is more preoccupied with what he does in his off-hours than with what he does at work? Why is there no explanation of the fact that his home address and his current place of business are 3,000 miles apart?

Why do we need his height and weight? Many people include this information, but the reason for doing so is obscure. Is he applying for a part in a television series about airline stewardesses, or submitting statistics for a dating bureau? What is the purpose? Who cares?

His education suggests he is bright . . . but he never finished his MBA, despite his year after year attempt. If he felt this graduate work was important, he might have worded his description of it differently, mentioning it at the end instead of at the beginning of his resumé:

I did graduate work in Business and Economics (perhaps naming a few of the courses and some of the professors) at the Zurich School of Economics in Zurich, Switzerland, and at the Universities of Chicago and California at Davis, off and on between the years 1953 and 1964.

He should allow the news about doing so well at Stamford to stand alone. It is good strong important data and should not be diluted with the additional graduate school drop-out information.

As for the rest of it, the material tells nothing about the person whose resumé it is except that he had nine jobs in twenty-five years and there are several peculiar gaps and overlaps in time along the way. We haven't the slightest idea what he's good at, what the skills and experience he is selling are. There is nothing which reveals what he has done in the past. The resumé is full of words and phrases which mean nothing or anything: "management planner," "project coordinator," "manager of administration." One comes away thinking he is more interested in hiding information about his past than in revealing it, because he omits relevant data.

How many people worked for him?

For what work was he responsible at any given time?

Did he accomplish anything? If so, what?

This is a bad resumé. It will fail to favorably impress a potential employer.

Controlling the Job Campaign

Because you are a housewife and because most businessmen do not have any understanding of what a housewife does or the imagination to figure out how these skills can be used by the business world, you must retain control over all aspects of your job campaign. That way you can explain your competence to the proper person at the time you have selected. That is why you must retain control over the way your resumé is used and who sees it.

Don't send your resumé in advance of your visit (unless

you already have an appointment with a hiring manager and he has requested to see it), unless you don't care what happens to it and have a high tolerance for wasted effort.

The moment an envelope leaves your hands it is out of your control. Any good salesman will tell you control of the sales process is vital to making a sale. You have to give up your resumé some time, but the later it happens in your campaign, the better the chances it will be used to your advantage.

You must leave your resumé behind after you have been interviewed. When you do this, it serves to buttress the favorable impression you have made in the interview.

You must remember the advice which may be appropriate for others is not necessarily good for you. The product you are offering is different and you mustn't care if everybody else sends out resumés as if they were circulation letters from *Time* magazine. Because your product is unusual, you must have personal contact in order to sell it properly.

You must be able to tell what you're good at and persuade your interviewer you are a valuable and resourceful potential employee. You must personally deliver this information because part of the message lies in the assertive way you have gone about designing your job campaign. (This is one of the ways you demonstrate your resourcefulness and determination.) If you send the resumé in *cold* (nobody has asked to see it) and *blind* (you don't know what's going to happen to it), it is as if you were dropping it languidly from the penthouse window. Don't treat this precious document with such profligacy.

People in the know may tell you you must send your resumé to hundreds of companies because surveys have shown any direct mail promotion automatically receives a return of 1 percent, no matter what the product or who the market. One percent of two hundred letters is a big two responses. Even more dismal intelligence is that most likely these two responses will be form letter "no interest" messages. All that work and postage and you won't have moved yourself any closer to an interview. The direct mail theory is a crock. Don't bother with it.

Don't be intimidated by people who talk knowledgeably

about a "broadcast" letter, either. A broadcast letter is a resumé written in paragraph form which extolls the writer's achievements and mentions he is looking to lend his superior competence to the addressee's company. When broadcast letters work, as they do occasionally, there are special reasons why and they don't necessarily apply to you. Sometimes a high-level executive who has had considerable visible management experience and an orderly progression of top-flight management jobs gets an interview with the person (a stranger) who receives the letter. The interview may happen as a courtesy. One executive will do a favor for another executive who is temporarily down on his luck, even if he isn't personally acquainted with him, because of his classy background. Someday the broadcast letter writer may be employed and then in a position to return the favor. The situation is not comparable to yours. Before meeting you no executive believes you will ever be in a position to help him. A resumé or broadcast letter slipped gratuitously over the transom is the method used by a supplicant, anyway, and that is definitely not the image you are creating. No resumé, no letter, no matter how eloquent and thoughtfully constructed, can, by itself, project the image you want.

Sometimes you will be tempted to send a copy of your resumé to someone you already know, when there is no immediate prospect of an interview. Your friend has learned you are looking for a job and has suggested you send it to him. That happens all the time. It may happen as a result of a cocktail party conversation or one in front of the beer section at the A & P, and it is unlikely anything at all will happen as a result of your sending him your resumé, generous and friendly as his impulse is when he asks for it. He will end up feeling guilty and you embarrassed. He will skim it over and pass it along to someone else as fast as he can (probably in the personnel department) who will write you a nice letter about how "Charles Jones has asked us to consider your resumé and although we have nothing available at present for someone with your background and qualifications, we will keep the material on file, etc. . . ."

You must use Charles Jones as a *contact*. Your purpose in

meeting with him is to get referrals to people he knows and you don't. You should not waste him by sending him a resumé and sitting back and waiting for *him* to do something about it. You must be the actor in this little drama. Businessmen, even ones who are friends of yours, often think of housewives as pleasant, nice little creatures who are "good sports." You can translate "good sports" as "patient and passive." That should give you a pretty good idea of why businessmen aren't falling all over each other to hire housewives. Passivity is not a quality businessmen respect in other businessmen. Why should they respect you because you're passive? You must demonstrate your ability to act and you will do that by calling Charles Jones and making an appointment to see him in his office. Cut short your conversation at the A & P by telling him you will call him *at the office*. Be friendly and pleasant and business-like. Do not loiter, permitting him to reinforce his stereo-type of you (a lady whose business it is to go grocery shopping).

His presence at the supermarket is an aberration (notice how he self-consciously explains his presence), so you must remove yourself from the setting if you want him to think of you in any other way.

Using What You Know

Without thoughtful examination of yourself and what you've done and what your objectives are, without considering these experiences in relation to your goals, you cannot write a resumé, cannot plan and control a job campaign, or select an appropriate career and earn a job offer. Self-knowledge is the key element in the whole process. It's a difficult undertaking, no question about it, and it is not for sissies. But, if you are not willing to take the trouble, then you may have to be content with life in a fantasy world of constant and poignant reiterations of "if only." Nobody but you is in charge of your future; you can control your past to the extent you select and present the information on the resumé you write for yourself, and the way you use this information in the conversations you have with potential employers.

You can control your future by analyzing and selecting the possibilities open to you.

It is a challenge, certainly. When you do these things in honest ways, presenting your side the way you want it presented, you may feel some pride in the achievement. You should. It's a hard job, worth the effort.

CHAPTER FOUR

Your Marketing Plan

A MARKETING PLAN ORCHESTRATES ACTIONS LEADING to and compelling sales. In an elegant retail store, marketing encompasses all the plans for the fall fashion lines, including the theme unifying the newspaper advertising with the various promotions, like the models who wander in and out of the store restaurant wearing different outfits and carrying little price cards. Sales and discount come-ons are also part of the seasonal marketing plan. Marketing comes in advance of sales and it is a plan determining emphasis and thrust of the sales campaign. In your job search, your marketing effort is directed to the selection, arrangement and use of its various elements. Of primary importance will be the contact you make with people who are in a position to help you. These contacts will be persons who are already known to you, as well as those you haven't met yet. You will make contact after you understand the purpose of the conversation you will have with them and how best to approach them.

In this planning phase of your job campaign, it is important to remember you need take only one step at a time. While you are organizing yourself, setting priorities, understanding your goals, your style and aptitudes, while you are preparing your *ideal job description* and writing your *resumé* and checking out the library, it is easy to become overwhelmed with the enormity of it all. There *is* a lot to do. Even with such an important objective—what you're going to be doing for the next twenty years—it is human to procrastinate. List making often becomes justification for doing nothing else and even takes the place of doing what you're talking about doing. Try to get through the making of lists as rapidly as you can for this reason.

When your program gets rolling, it is likely you will be able to accomplish several things every day. Keep it easy on yourself in the beginning, though. You don't want to scare yourself into paralysis.

Identifying Your Market

You have in hand your *ideal job description;* you know the actions you enjoy taking. You have limited your ambition realistically to those activities you enjoy and do well. In this way you have strengthened and focused your ambition. You have visited the library and poked around and come up with occupations holding the tasks and functions you have identified as those of interest to you. You have been able to discover what fields are likely to offer the occupations you are pointing toward. Next, you will devise a method by which you can make contact with a buyer. There are several such methods. Let's go first with the people you know.

Personal Contacts

As you've learned, most management job hiring comes about because of personal contacts. This means the job offer comes through someone already known to you or known to somebody you know. Personal contact must be exploited thoroughly because this activity produces the best odds.

It makes sense to design a plan of action based on the law of probabilities.

One of the reasons the "old school tie" or the "club" has

always been so important to male management is that good old Harry can serve as an important introduction into a coveted inner sanctum, just as he is a dependable source of corporate gossip and is likely to know places in need of new people before everybody else knows it. An early foot in the door is an advantage. This kind of knowledge runs across the board and covers all working classes. Uncle Harry may be a member of the exclusive Union Club or the backbone of the Wednesday night bowling league; the point is he represents the most personal kind of entrée into a place which otherwise would be inaccessible.

This referral system has worked well, over the years, for the business establishment, particularly in notoriously closed circles like banks and investment houses, where crass, aggressive behavior (like letters coming unbidden from people unknown to the letters' recipients) is frowned upon. A personal introduction to the right person remains an extremely valuable tool and our friends in the gray pin stripes have understood this for a long time.

One of the nice things happening since the Second World War is the inner circle has inexorably widened (against its will) because the population has grown so dramatically and because upwardly mobile and other unusual types (like women) have demanded entry into heretofore sacred and inaccessible territories. The business introduction withheld patronizingly from your grandmother will, most probably, be offered to you *if you ask for it*. Doors are just not locked as tightly against unusual kinds of intrusions as they once were.

It is true middle management all over the country is depressingly top-heavy with white males. We women may not sit on the corporate boards of directors in the numbers we should, but time has never been riper for those of us who are so inclined to make demands.

Many men are feeling self-conscious about the discrimination against women that has gone on for so long. You can take advantage of that low-level guilt feeling without mentioning it. Others of these self-conscious persons are men who *don't* admit to feeling guilty for a moment and are even in favor of a continuation of this unequal status-quo. Asking a favor from this kind of person won't necessarily turn out badly, either. He can't imagine the world will ever change to the extent man's role will be in jeopardy, so he is gracious and magnanimous and condescending when it is a matter of one-on-one personal contact.

As in so much else in this world, your technique is as important to achieving goals as is the substance of your approach.

1. *Who do you know?* Let's talk about the personal contacts you are going to make in your job search.

By the time you have reached the age of thirty-five, you are personally acquainted with hundreds of people. Maybe thousands of acquaintances you've made in addition to your close friendships. These relationships are disparate. They range from your favorite cashier at the check-out counter at the supermarket, to your pharmacist, to the children's crossing guard, to the man who sits behind the polished mahogany desk at the bank. Your doctor may or may not be someone you invite to your house for dinner, but he knows you and you know him. Parents of the children in your children's classes, members of your garden club, husbands of the members of your garden club, sons of the members of your garden club, business friends of your husband, people who live down the block to whom you've spoken sometimes when you've seen them out raking leaves in their yards. If you made a list of your acquaintances, you could probably come up with the names of eighty or so people and you wouldn't need to pause more than a couple of times. When it comes to your close friends, you can probably add another ten or twelve names. No matter how isolated you believe yourself to be, you have not been a recluse.

These people represent the personal contacts available to you; they know people who know people. Circles around circles around circles, each connected to each other circle. You must use your list, learn what to say to the people you know well and what to say to the people you know less well, so your objective of meeting and interviewing people who will be able to offer you a job is achieved. The people you will contact are those people who go to work every day or know well people who go to work every day. Most of these people will be men.

It's the same way old Harry's nephew (at the Club) uses his relationship with Harry by announcing, "Hey, Unk, now that I've got my degree in Oriental caligraphy from the Rhode Island School of Design, I think I'd like to go to work on Wall Street." And Uncle Harry responds, as Uncle Harrys always have, "Well, if you'll get a haircut and polish those godawful army shoes, I'll just call up Undercut Peabody the Third and make an appointment for you. I've heard the bank is putting in an entry-level training program one of his assistants is heading up."

Always remember you (the housewife) are coming from an alien place separated from the Uncle Harrys of the world; you must continually remind him you are able— even eager—to do things for yourself. Harry's nephew may be permitted the luxury of sitting back while Harry does the telephoning for him because in these circles *everybody* got his start this way (before the days of college recruiting), but you can't permit anyone to do this for you. You must prove your active commitment to your goal, not through talking about it but demonstrating it in the most basic and obvious ways.

An additional difficulty arises which is a circumstance peculiar to your particular situation. You must couple the necessary active control of your job search with an awareness that asking somebody for a job is very threatening, even aggressive behavior. A frontal attack which combines your assertiveness with a request for a job is too much for most people to handle unless you achieve an exquisite balance between an expression of your needs and the fears of the people with whom you talk. Let me elucidate.

If you go to one of your contacts, someone who is seeing you as a personal favor, and say, "I want a job," or "Please give me a job," or act as if that is what you're saying even if you don't actually say the words, it won't work. This demand puts the person to whom you're talking in a passive mode where he is being acted *upon* and he doesn't like that a bit. He wants to be a manly, decision-making fellow, who acts on the lives of other people, not the other way around.

Moreover, the demand, which is an outgrowth of your

helplessness, reminds him of his own vulnerability. His immediate response is "I can't help you. I don't have a job for you. Please go away. Your presence here makes me uncomfortable and reminds me I am not nearly so secure and powerful and in charge of things as I like to think I am." Your plea embarrasses him; it makes him sweat. In order to reassert his control over the situation, he may offer to help you write your resumé or to give you advice. But if you ask him for a job, if you reveal your own feelings of desperation, the meeting will be a cold and unrewarding one.

Most of us find it difficult to make eye contact with panhandlers and feel mysteriously threatened by them. People in power often have trouble with people who are out of power, even when they are normally compassionate and tenderhearted. When a person feels threatened, the usual response is a negative one.

2. *You are not allowed to ask for a job.* You may not be aware of it, but that rule puts you in a fortunate position. You haven't worked for pay in several years and most of the people you know, know it. The reason this is fortunate is you can go to see people who work in management positions *ostensibly* to ask for guidance. Who needs advice more than you? Had you been working all this time, you wouldn't deserve—or receive—special consideration.

People are always glad to talk about how they've gotten where they've gotten, to explain some of the idiosyncracies about their jobs, their companies, their industries. They aren't threatened when people ask them, sincerely, to talk about themselves. They like also to flex their muscles a little by telling the less-blessed others what they should be doing in order to achieve similar successes. Since you are a mere housewife, it is evident to these people you will need a lot of help and advice. As long as you do not act like a supplicant by asking straight-out for a job, people will tend to be generous with their time and what they regard as their expertise.

You will have to exercise control over the conversation so that you will come away from the meeting with the names of others to whom you will be able to talk. If every person with whom you meet gives you the name of at least one other person, and probably more, you can see you will be busy for several months just following up your initial appointments.

Your chances are eight in ten one of those people down the line will have a job for you. In order to earn these referrals, you must ask good questions and talk coherently and persuasively about your skills. The person with whom are you talking may start out by presuming you are ignorant about business; giving you the names of others to contact *with permission to use his name* means you have met your objective. He is not afraid you will "come on too strong" with his friends or embarrass him in some other way. It means he trusts you to represent him competently. You have behaved in a straightforward, businesslike way with him and that was your objective.

The way to get people you know well to see you (always in their offices) is to call them up on the telephone and ask them. The way to disarm them and ask them for an appointment without being threatening to them with blatant beggary is to say, "I am exploring the job market (looking into, making a study of, talking to people about, etc.). *While I have no reason to believe you have a job, or even know about one,* I am interested in finding out what you think about the opportunities in the information industry, especially for someone who has experience in organizing and writing reports, as I have." Say whatever you want (quoting freely from your resumé *objective*), as long as you put the disclaimer (*"I have no reason to believe . . ."*) right up front. It is the truth, after all. You know no job is going to fall from the sky after one phone call and one office visit, anyway. The rest of the telephone conversation depends on your style, your relationship with the person to whom you are talking and how you feel that day. In any event, keep it short and to the point. You must demonstrate your first gentle assertiveness by suggesting you will be in the neighborhood of his office on such and such an afternoon, how does four o'clock sound? Do not shrink from this task. You have nothing to lose and no one is going to think less of you. This is exactly what people who are serious about rustling up a job for themselves do when they are confident of their own value.

The purpose of this first phone call is to set up an

appointment with someone with whom you feel comfortable. (Do three or four easy ones first, then start approaching the people you know less well. You'll soon get into a good, relaxed approach and technique.)

When you make the appointment, you will tell your friend that you plan on talking with him in his office for twenty or thirty minutes, at most. Your telephone manner will be pleasant and businesslike, a preview of your appointment demeanor, *no matter how long you have known one another.* Remember, he must shift gears about you and learn to adjust his thinking so he can picture you in an office. You must help him come to grips with your new identity. Your telephone manner should not be too crisp or brusque: It will be straightforward and concise. Write it out first, if you wish. That often helps.

3. *Your conversation must be a dialogue.* When you visit your friend in his office, you must repeat your disclaimer (use the same words, if you wish—he'll never remember what you said on the phone). You can permit him to lead the initial small talk if that is comfortable for you. Before it gets too personal or too casual, bring it to a businesslike subject. You can do that if you remember to keep the purpose of the meeting in front of you.

> Present yourself as an intelligent, skilled and resourceful person with your feet on the ground (so he is willing to introduce you to a business associate);
>
> Obtain names of business associates from him who are not personally known to you, in order to contact them *using his name.*

As long as you remember your purpose, you can permit him to talk about his own career, or his company, or to give you advice. When he asks you questions about yourself (and he will, sooner or later, or he will ask, "What can I do for you?" which is really the same thing), you must respond in a relaxed way, using the action verbs you've pulled together in your resume. Any questions sounding as if they are prompted by his curiosity about what it is you think you can do can be answered in the same general way: "In the past few years, I've developed communications and developmental skills. In my work as a contributor to the PTA newsletter, I've done research in the area of nutrition and its relationship to the learning process, and have communicated some of this information through articles I've written for the newsletter." Crib it straight from your resumé; he doesn't know yet what it says.

You can continue with a statement like "I'm curious to know how my skills as a writer and researcher can be transferred to the business world. *What kinds of writing and research gets done in a company like yours? Do you have a house organ? What kinds of articles are the people who work here interested in reading? Is there an advertising copywriting department? I'm interested in knowing about your company. How did you get your start?*" (Of course, you don't hit him in the face with a barrage of questions. Place them diplomatically throughout the conversation. Otherwise he will hide under his desk.)

Always remember to disarm him. After all, you're not asking him for a job . . . "Of course it's early in my job search. I expect it will take five or six months before I find a place I suit that suits me." When he asks again, toward the end of the visit, what he can do for you, be frank. Tell him you'd like to meet with people with whom he is acquainted to pursue the same general topic. You know it is unlikely they will know of job opportunities either, but since you are serious about your exploration of the job market (you have, after all, *twenty or thirty years ahead of you in which you plan to pursue a career in business*) you are deeply interested in finding out about different organizations and the people in them. All you want from him are names of people like him. Your friend need do nothing whatever after you leave his office. The other bad part about asking somebody to help you find a job is he will feel desperately guilty if he doesn't do something he says he's going to do and of course he won't because even the most loving people are lazy and careless about promises, especially when there's nothing in it for them. Leave nothing to chance, nothing to someone else's *largesse*. You are in charge and in control of your job search. If somebody else does the calling or the appointment making, you will be on the defensive with the stranger who has been contacted in this manner the moment you walk through his office door. That makes you the helpless little darling, which is about 180 degrees from the image you have been constructing so carefully. The man whom Bill calls will be doing nothing but a favor for good old Bill, if it is good old Bill who sets up the appointment. At your approach the stranger's eyes will glaze and harden because that's the way people get when they've been roped into something. When you call and speak to him and he makes an appointment with you under his own volition, then neither of you will have to be defensive later. He likes to be in control of his own decisions, too. He will be curious to find out about you and he will be curious because he has already listened to you on the telephone. He has chosen to talk to you in person. No one twisted his arm. He could have turned you down, but he did not. That's important. Very few sales presentations turn out well if the audience is captive or resentful or in some way unwilling to listen.

When you telephone your friend's referral, you say exactly the same thing you said originally to your friend *except* you introduce yourself and explain that "Bill Smith suggested I get in touch with you . . ." The introduction of a name known to your listener makes him less suspicious (and gets you past the ever-protective secretary, as a rule). It also makes it probable he will share some time with you. ". . . and while he gave me no reason to believe you have a job available, or even know about one, he said you were knowledgeable about . . . and it would be beneficial for me to talk with you."

When you talk to this second-generation contact, your purpose is precisely what it was when you spoke to good old Bill: appearing businesslike and competent and getting more referrals. Never take more than half an hour of anyone's time for this kind of meeting (unless the chat turns into an interview for a specific job, which will happen, happily, on occasion), and never permit the conversation to become flirtatious.

Many men still feel uncomfortable with strange women in places other than living rooms and cocktail lounges, and some of them fall naturally into the "Me-Tarzan, you-Jane" attitude. (He may wonder what he is supposed to say to some strange woman who is not a secretary. Perhaps he even thinks you are Bill's *mistress*.) You can smile pleasantly and ask him about the interests he has that brought him to this position in this company. If your questions clearly spring from an impersonal curiosity and desire to find out, he will respond in kind and forget the other stuff. Men really aren't jungle animals. It's just they were never taught how to deal with women as equals. They have no experience with it. Maybe you don't, either. Keep talking quietly and pleasantly and remain cool, so he can take the lead from you. It may turn out to be one of the most gratifying conversations *he* ever had.

Keep a record of your appointments and a brief description of what transpired, including a general description of the conversation, and a list of the referrals you receive. If you didn't get any referrals, note that and see if you can figure out why. This is important because it will help you sort it out so it doesn't happen often.

If, for example, you got the bum's rush or it all happened so fast you never had time to ask for a referral, figure out why that occurred and how something you could have done or said might have changed it. Perhaps it seemed impolite or inappropriate for you to ask for names; the opportunity just never arose. Maybe he never asked what he could do for you, perhaps you waited for his permission so you could ask him. Note whatever happened in your record of the meeting and devise a better script for that particular situation when it comes up again. After an unsuccessful episode, you must ask yourself where it went wrong. Did you get into Bridge Club conversation and forget the purpose of the appointment? Examine what was said in the meeting as soon afterwards as you can. This documentation of your appointments is your job search *log*. You keep it as faithfully and diligently as does a ship's captain. This will help you see what went wrong and what went right in your interviews. You can change tactics if it looks as if you should, if, for example, you are consistently failing to get referrals. You can note also what you're doing correctly, study that and see how you can integrate successful experiences into *every* presentation.

After every appointment, whether it is first generation or second, third or fourth, you will leave your resumé at the conclusion of the conversation. Your comments during the appointment have purposely followed the text of the resumé; when the recipient scans the material after you've left and before he drops it in his "out" basket for his secretary to file, the information will serve to buttress his impression of you and lock in the memory of it: The purpose of the resumé, left in this way, is to *positively reinforce* his memory of the meeting. No more than two days later you must write him and thank him for meeting with you. The reason for doing this as quickly as possible is he may, then, still have your resumé on his desk or in his drawer. That means he will attach the letter to the resumé *himself*— another opportunity for positive reinforcement.

As for the thank-you letter, it must be written in an understated, non-gushy manner. Include few adjectives and no adverbs and *type it*. Typing is important. If you don't have a typewriter, beg, steal or borrow one. If you send a handwritten note, no matter how lovely and artistic your handwriting is, it will not strengthen the businesslike image you have designed and it may detract from it. Remember you are engaged in a sophisticated marketing plan, no less important to you than to companies which spend millions of dollars designing their corporate logo, selecting appropriate stationery and type face for every typewriter in the place. All this is done to convey a particular corporate image. Your plan must include your own sophistication as part of the image you are projecting. Remember, too, most businessmen have handwriting resembling the undeciferable part of the Rosetta Stone; if your handwriting is decent, it will serve only to to put more distance between you. If you have awful handwriting, writing a letter using it may not put distance between you and him, but it won't communicate anything, either, if he can't read it.

If you can't type, find someone who can (people who type usually have their own typewriters) and make some kind of arrangement whereby you can get letters typed quickly and on a regular basis. If you must handwrite the letters, do so only if you are *convinced* there is no other alternative.

Make sure your stationery is plain white or cream

color—*no pretty flowers, bumble bees or butterflies.* It is nice to have a letterhead with your name and address printed on it, but not necessary.

Your letter should be three paragraphs in length: The first paragraph should thank the person for giving you an opportunity to meet with him and for the interesting (fruitful, stimulating—your *Roget's Thesaurus* can be used here as well as for your resumé) discussion. The second paragraph should amplify or set straight some aspect of the discussion you had. (This is a good place to correct any mistakes you made—don't admit they were mistakes, though—or to emphasize an important point you think should be stressed.) This paragraph should be three or four sentences long.

The last paragraph in the letter should reiterate your appreciation for the meeting *and* mention you will soon be in touch with the people to whom he referred you (mention them by name if there are no more than two). Tell him you will keep him apprised of the progress you make on your job search (even if he didn't refer you to anyone or act particularly interested. This is no place for false pride.). The letter is gracious and concise. Rely on the use of declarative sentences. That will help you refrain from sounding gushy or pretentious.

Do what you say you're going to do: Every three or four weeks, drop him a note (typewritten, of course) telling how you're doing, to whom you've been talking especially if you have spoken with one or more of his referrals, some of the interesting insights you've gained. Act *as if* he is interested, even if he is a third- or fourth-generation contact. It is better to write than to call if the message contains information about the status of your job search (it provides an opportunity for more tangible reinforcement by demonstrating your good organization and ability to follow through). If you have a question, you can include that in the letter and then follow up on the phone.

Be guided by your common sense. Your objective with each letter you write is to appear businesslike and well organized.

Here are three examples of thank-you letters. The first one goes to your original contact, friend Bill Smith, after you have met with him. The next letter goes to Bill Smith's referral, Al Grant, after you have interviewed him. The third letter goes to Bill Smith, keeping him informed of the progress of your job campaign and telling him about your meeting with his friend, Al Grant.

Dear Bill:

I appreciate very much your generosity in meeting and talking with me on Monday. Your interest is gratifying.

Since communications and public relations represent areas in which I plan to use the skills I have developed, your suggestion to talk to people at the Milwaukee Publicity Club was a good one. I have discovered the group has a monthly luncheon meeting downtown and the president of the club has invited me to attend the next one.

Thank you for referring me to Tom Cooke and Al Grant. I plan to call them early next week, then let you know how the conversations go. I will also keep you apprised of the progress of my exploration. Thanks again for meeting with me.

Cordially,

Dear Al Grant:

I appreciate very much your generosity in taking time on Thursday to meet and talk with me.

It was interesting to learn of the possibilities for development of communication programs in an industrial company such as yours. People who are skilled at writing clear explanations of the way things work are important to the company's to-the-public and to-its-employees communications efforts, especially when the product is as complex as yours.

I was particularly interested in the internal newsletter you were kind enough to show me. I have been in
touch with its editor, David Morton, as you suggested, and plan to see him early next week. Thank you
again for sharing your time with me. I will keep you
informed of the progress of my job search and discovery.

Sincerely yours,

Dear Bill:

I met with Al Grant day before yesterday and found him
to be a straightforward, no-nonsense kind of person,
as you had described. He was extremely helpful, even
to the point of taking me for a brief walk through the
plant. He was additionally helpful by suggesting I
get in touch with the editor of their internal newsletter, which I am in the process of doing.

Al Grant is precisely the kind of person I want to talk
with; he understands the necessity of a company like
Computer World, Inc., having a clearly enunciated
public stance, as well as appropriate and up-to-the-
minute internal and external communications. These
are areas in which I would be able to make a contribution.

I have been unable to make contact yet with Tom Cooke,
who has been out of the country. I am continuing the
effort and thank you again.

Cordially,

All of this communications activity helps to make
certain each person will continue to be involved in your
search and it will give them the maximum opportunity to
help you. If the lines of communication between you
continue to be healthy (and this is largely up to you), when
they have an idea about someone you should talk to, or an

opening they have lately become aware of, they can get in touch with you without feeling self-conscious. This way, they will continue to be of value to you, even after you have left their offices. An orderly program of follow-up comunication is nearly as important as the initial contact because that is how you can best take advantage of "second thoughts" and unexpected, later knowledge. Every person who makes his living selling knows the value of maintaining contacts.

Starting with somebody you know, there are, at most, only five people between you and an introduction to anybody in the world. If you are by nature fearless and without self-consciousness, with unlimited money and time, you may be able to arrange to meet Paul Newman or the president of United Technology. Most of us are less inclined to go through the machinations producing such an introduction (what do you do then?) but you've seen the friends and acquaintances you have can lead you quite directly to your ultimate objective, which is meeting with a person who will make you a job offer.

Other Kinds of Contacts

You will want to make contact with other people, *hiring managers,* who are not known to you personally, or to your friends. *Insurance* contacts. These contacts are less likely to lead you to pay dirt, but if you are of a compulsive nature, it is likely you will not want to leave a stone unturned.

These other, *insurance* contacts, may head a department where you'd like to work; the hiring and firing of people who report to them is their responsibility. They work in a discipline in which you are interested, in a field in which you are interested.

1. *Cold calls.* One way to find out who the various directors and managers of the functions you're interested in is to call the company and ask who they are, by the titles you assume they have. ("Please give me the name of your West Coast Distribution Manager." "Who handles purchasing for all of the U.S. Widget facilities in this location?") You are not interested in finding out the names of

the presidents or vice presidents of large corporations.
They will be listed in the directories you find in the library,
anyway *(Standard & Poor's, The Dun and Bradstreet Million Dollar
Directory, The Advertisers' Red Book)*. You are interested in
middle-level managers who are not important enough to
be included in the major directories' listings. They are the
people who are in a position to hire you. Information as to
who and where they are and what they call themselves is
available to you over the telephone. Usually, the switchboard operator will give you the names without any fuss.
Sometimes, however, she will put you right into the
department itself and somebody will pick up the phone
before you are prepared to deal with anybody except the
operator. Assume this person is a secretary or a functionary of some kind—not the boss. Bosses don't normally
answer the phone. Ask the name and title of the person in
charge of the department. That is not classified information and you will probably get it. If the phone-answerer
gets nudgy and asks why you want to know, you can say
you are writing him a letter and want the proper spelling of
his name and his exact title. Never reveal to an underling
you are looking for a job. Underlings try to protect their
bosses from such demands and tend to act very smug to
boot. So say you are writing the manager a letter. You're
doing research, you want some information for a report
you're writing.

If they still don't tell you, give up. There are plenty of
other fish in the sea.

The telephone is a wonderful instrument, it affords an
anonymous way of obtaining useful information. Out
there on the other end, nobody knows who you are,
whether or not you're wearing lipstick or have been to the
beauty parlor. You have no name, no face and you can hang
up at any time, whenever you want, even if it is rude.
People always answer the telephone (can you let one ring
even when you are in somebody's house and know it isn't
for you?). If you are courteous and friendly, know what
you want and if you keep it simple, if you are unhurried and
assume help is forthcoming, it usually is. Your warmth and
trustworthiness are almost always rewarded.

Incidentally, most men have a weakness for strange

women who call them on the telephone, no matter how they feel about women who want to join their bowling and softball leagues. While you must never use your voice in an overt sexual way, à la Marilyn Monroe or Marlene Dietrich, the very fact you are female is enough for most men, and they will tell you whatever you want to know, if it's not classified information. If you sound intelligent, that's a real bonus. So speak quietly, firmly and smile when you speak. This last may make you feel silly, but it will add warmth to your voice. It has been my experience that a man is much more likely to help me when I call in *cold* over the telephone than a woman is in the same circumstances. Chalk it up to the wonders and mysteries of sex, but hope a man answers.

Another way to find out who holds what title is to go to the company itself. If it is housed in a big office building, very likely there is a listing in the lobby of people's names, titles and floor locations. If the titles are not listed in the lobby directory, write down some of the names and floor numbers that are listed. You can telephone these people and ask them (or their secretaries) what their titles are. If it turns out they are not the people you want, ask them who *is* the Director of Training and Development. They have a company telephone directory at their elbow and they can look up the information for you.

If you have decided you would like to work in the university office dealing with financial aid to students, you call the university and find out who is in charge of financial assistance. It may take several phone calls (they may think you're after a loan), but you will get the proper name if you persevere. Don't forget to ask to whom you are speaking as you make the various connections; you might find out you're talking to someone in a department you are equally curious about. This kind of telephone research gives you an additional feel for the organization, especially if you talk to several people. The time of day affects the kind of conversations you are likely to have, too. If you call after five or five-thirty, most probably the phone will be picked up by someone in management, as opposed to a secretary. You may find this an advantage, depending on the kind of information you're after (it is possible you may want to check out other information about a company besides names and titles of people). Also, offices tend to empty out at lunchtime except for the person eating yogurt at her desk. Bear that in mind. Be aware, too, that people who are at work at eight in the morning are a breed apart. Call them workaholics if you must and figure out what kind of approach, if any, is appropriate for people like them. A person who comes in early may do so in order to get work done and to *avoid* telephone calls. They may greet your call without enthusiasm. It is probably better to leave them alone.

Think of yourself as a detective. You are ferreting out the names of people you may end up interviewing. The more names you discover, the better it is for you. If you live in a city, I would say an initial list of ten to fifteen names will be sufficient for your first barrage.

2. *Query letters.* You are going to write each of them a *query letter.* This is a letter which asks for information. *When letters ask for information which is within the recipient's knowledge, he feels obligated to answer it.* For example: If I were to write a letter to the president of the First National Bank and say, "I like money, I like banks. I want a job. Will you hire me?"—I would never get a response from him. Even though I asked a question in the letter, it is not a legitimate question because the person I have addressed has no concern about or interest in the subject. He may send my letter to the personnel department (and you know what I think of that) so I will get some impersonal thumbs-down form letter response. But no good will come of my letter. A real *query letter* is one in which the letter's writer seeks information the addressee can legitimately, as part of his job, give out. Here are two basic rules to follow when writing a query letter:

State who you are
and your purpose for writing.

Don't weasle around with some smarmy sentence about "you don't know me and I don't know you, etc." Business letters often go between people who have never met one another. A *query letter* has nothing whatever to do with a social letter. The same rules do not apply.

Remember your purpose.

The most important objective you have in writing this letter is to convey both your intelligence and your interest in the addressee's organization. You don't expect the person to whom you are writing to drop everything and command his subordinates to "hire this woman!" That would be unrealistic. You want a favorable response so you can respond to the answer and ultimately gain an interview.

Here is a sample *query letter*. Notice it tells immediately who the writer is.

Dear Mr. Robbins:

I have been a housewife and mother for the past fourteen years, since I attended (graduated from) the University of Kansas. During these years I have developed an interest in computers and information systems, due in part to several courses in that field I've taken at the Westfalia Community College.

I am writing to you because I am exploring the various options available to knowledgeable beginners in this field. Your company has an outstanding reputation and I decided you would be an excellent source for answers to some of the questions I have. My curiosity focuses on the role of Computer, Inc., in the specialized area of computerized information services provided to libraries, an area in which I have deep interest. While I have no reason to believe you have a position available, or even know about one appropriate for someone with my unconventional background and experience, I am curious about the use of computer terminals in research libraries, both public and private. I will be grateful for information about this aspect of Computer, Inc.'s business.

Such data will be helpful to me as I decide which area of this exciting field I will move into.

I look forward to hearing from you.

Sincerely yours,

You can also ask, if you wish, about the training or orientation programs a company has for newcomers, particularly the unusual kind of newcomer you represent.

If you are interested in working for a newspaper in your community, you might write to an editor or an assistant publisher and ask if there are surveys about whether most newspaper reporters are graduates of schools of journalism, or what is this particular newspaper's policy about the use of stringers vis-à-vis full-time reporters and writers. How much—if any—opportunity is there for a reporter to develop her own news speciality? Ask about the relationship of advertising revenue to editorial policy or whether "women's news" will ever become "hard" news. Let your curiosity direct your questions.

Another way to identify people to whom you want to write or to call is to keep track of people whose letters appear in the Letters to the Editor column. This is often a rich source of people with whom you'd like to correspond.

What a *query letter* must contain is evidence you already know something about the company, about the industry, or about the function within it. Your questions will spring from this prior knowledge (gained from poking around at the library and conversations with people who know about it).

If your purpose is to get a worthwhile reply to your *query letter*, you must have prior knowledge when you write it. When you do, you will appear intelligent because you *ask good questions*. The difference between a good question and a dumb question is that the smart one is based on a sensible if incomplete grasp of the matter; dumb questions come from left field. Good questions in a *query letter* always have a bearing on some aspect of how a company does business.

The person you write will probably answer the letter himself, or else he will forward it to someone else who can more appropriately field the questions you've asked. Remember you want the person who answers the letter to be the person with whom you will talk further; keep your query limited to the functional area in which you are interested, if possible. If the person you pick to write isn't the person you should be writing, the topic of your letter will dictate the proper person to respond to it.

After you get the hang of the *query letter,* you should write one a day, always keeping a carbon copy. Again, the letters must be typed. When you receive an answer, give the person a call: "Thank you for responding to my letter." (Discuss the reply briefly and then jump right in.)

"The reason I was curious about _____ is I'm exploring the job market and while I have no reason to believe you have a job or even know about one, I know you are knowledgeable about the growth and future (or etc.) of computers in public libraries. That is a field in which I am vitally interested and I would like to discuss general opportunities in the field with you. I am going to be in the neighborhood of your office on Tuesday afternoon. May I drop by then for a short conversation around three o'clock?"

Because no one has referred you, this is more of a hard sell than is the personal contact call, so it is generally not as successful. The fact you have written him a letter and *he has responded* is important leverage, however, not to be discounted. One out of four such people will ask you to send them your resumé. Go ahead, it can't hurt. Don't count on anything further happening though.

One in six will make an appointment and those interviews will be conducted just as I've described the second- and third-generation interviews. Your objective in such a meeting is to appear intelligent and well organized, *and* to get referrals.

About Classified Ads

You know my opinion about answering ads (see Chapter 2). If you must answer an ad, always do so at least a week after the ad has appeared in the newspaper. The odds of your letter and resumé being read carefully are greatest after some time has elapsed. An ad always produces the greatest influx of responses (your competition) the week it runs. You need special attention. Don't worry, jobs are *never* filled in a week, not the one you're after, anyhow.

Ads are not a particularly fruitful ground for reentering females. People who run ads generally want a pile of standard resumés to beef up their files and they won't know what to do with yours. For that reason, when you answer an ad, put one or two job titles which you're after in your covering letter. (The letter you send with your resumé telling which ad you are answering.) That way you will direct the action of the resumé reader, even (as is likely) if he doesn't call you for an interview. Because he doesn't have a whole lot of imagination, he will file you in the place you tell him to file you: "Product Manager," "Sales Representative," "Bookkeeper."

Ads are run for many reasons, only one of which is to locate appropriate persons to interview for a specific job. Sometimes ads are placed after a job has been filled on the qt, so as to comply with equal employment practices regulations, to demonstrate to the powers that be, "See, we ran this ad in good faith before Jim Mansfield, who is thirty-five years old, white and male, was named to it. There weren't any other appropriately qualified applicants, that's why we gave him the job. Too bad."

Sometimes ads describe fictitious jobs and are run merely to attract resumés (employment agencies periodically like to beef up their files in particular functions), or to attract customers who will use their services. There are all kinds of reasons to run ads and not too many good ones for answering them. However, a chance exists you will get an interview by responding to an ad (maybe one in fifteen). Since you don't want to ignore any possibility, by all means answer those ads which describe the job that makes you salivate.

Summary

Your marketing plan must be carefully organized. You have specific tasks following each other logically, one after another. The organization of the campaign includes:

1. Your list of personal contacts; their office addresses and their office telephone numbers.
2. Your *log*. The story of every interview in which you participate, including the name and address of the person with whom you spoke, his telephone number and the referrals he gave you. It may be easiest to keep this information on your index cards.
3. Your list of hiring managers; their addresses and telephone numbers (also on your index cards).
4. Copies of all of your letters: thank-you letters, queries, ad responses, the works.

When you meet with people, you must treat them with the same professional detachment as you have learned to treat yourself within the context of the job search. Detachment is not indifference.

When you know the rules of the game and apply them to your situation, it becomes easy to see the ways to win.

CHAPTER FIVE

The Interview

Your Sales Presentation

The interview is the sales presentation of your job campaign. You will make the presentation after you have prepared your resumé and have decided which aspects of your experience to emphasize.

Whether or not you have trouble with the interview depends on your attitude and your understanding of what you want, what you expect and how much clear thinking you are willing to do. Unemotional examination of any situation robs it of its mystery and, in turn, its capacity to produce fear.

Because the interview is your sales presentation, there is a specific and predictable ritual you will go through, as happens with any sales call. Preparation for the ritual begins long before you walk into an office (the contacts you make, the telephone calls, the letters, even the decision about the clothes you wear). Several things are likely to happen during the interview itself. There is a brief time at the beginning when you can expect to go through a "small talk" routine (a meaningless conversation meant, supposedly, to put the interviewee at ease). This period permits both of you to take each other's measure, in much the same way grunting and glowering and circling one another does in primitive societies when the men of different tribes or clans are introduced to each other. The nervousness one feels in advance of these modern encounters can be traced, I think, to this deeply subconscious curiosity about the unknown other person and what he represents. Civilization provides us with "small talk," as good a way as any to test and probe the other person without resorting to clubs and sticks.

You will talk about the weather, or how long it took you to get from someplace else to here (men are endlessly fascinated with transportation and the length of time it takes to get from one place to another, don't ask me why), and that exchange will last anywhere from a minute to fifteen minutes, depending on how good you both are at this kind of prattle. Since you are going to know what ground must be covered in the interview, you can signal your readiness to get on with it one of two ways. If it is a referral interview, one which you instigated and one to which the other person has agreed even though he does not necessarily have a job or know about one, you are the *interviewer*. You will smile and begin, easily and unthreateningly, to ask the questions you have decided to ask, in order to get the information and the referrals you want.

If this interview is for a specific job, your behavior and what you say will accommodate that fact: You will be the *interviewee*. As such, when you feel enough time has been spent in sniffing around at each other, you will indicate you are ready for serious business by pleasantly shortening your replies to his social questions. This will reveal your intention to get on with the matter at hand, and indicate that you are prepared for serious business.

A job interview is a mutual evaluation process wherein data is transmitted and received. It is a conversation, usually between two people, which has a particular purpose. It is not a social occasion. It is a business meeting and is no more difficult to manage, once you get the hang of it, than is any other interpersonal encounter.

Remind yourself nothing is magic. An interview can be reduced to a recipe, an uncomplicated series of steps and rules. It is not nearly so mysterious or as emotionally charged as a blind date, even though it holds many of the same terrors.

Your entire future does not hinge on the outcome of this particular meeting. This silly attitude only produces panic. By now you know panic is bad because it intrudes between rational thought and action. To prevent panic, it is necessary to sort out the emotional baggage producing it.

Job seeking hits you in your most vulnerable part: your self-esteem. If you're out of a job you feel worthless, even if you've been successfully running a household for many years. You feel even worse when you think you've been running a household *unsuccessfully* for many years; you think everybody on the bus is staring at you.

Yet you are not a stranger to interviewing. Parent-Teacher conferences are interviews. "Talks" with your children are, too. Every time you've hired anyone, from a piano teacher to a baby-sitter, you've participated in a job interview. The style of an interview can range from very casual and informal to highly structured, even stressful.

You control what you say at an interview because you know the purpose of the meeting and you can predict, therefore, what will be asked. An infusion of this practical reality will help you to straighten your spine.

Let's sort out some of the feelings bombarding the job seeker as she trembles apprehensively in the outer office.

QUESTION: What do you feel, sitting outside in the waiting room awaiting the interview?

ANSWER: Like a supplicant, with all the negative images that word conveys. You feel like a beggar.

The stranger (almost always a man) sitting in his important office has something you want (a job which will pay you money) and the only way he will give it to you is if you *please* him. Because you feel unworthy of this bounty (you are *inexperienced*), it is as if you were asking for a gift, a favor given you only because this philanthropist decides to bestow his generosity upon you. You are as a little girl once again, asking for a new dress because you are incapable of providing it for yourself. The power lies in the hands of the person to whom you are talking: *You* are powerless. It is a familiar feeling. You unconsciously imitate those other times in your past when you pleased a person who had the power to grant you something you wanted very much.

"Oh, how smart you are, I never could have done that myself."

"What a lovely big office, you must have worked very hard to get to be so important."

Familiar behavior roles are the easiest to fall into even if they are not appropriate. Making somebody else feel good by denegrating one's own competence or importance is not appropriate in a job interview.

Rules of the Game

The first rule in an interview: *Detach.*

Think of yourself as a product. A jar of cold cream. An aspirin tablet. It is much easier if people reject your product instead of you. If they don't like your arm, well, it's your *arm.* It's part of you. It is difficult not to take such rejection personally. But if it is a cake of soap you've offered and he's turned down, you can look over the cake of soap, talk about what he wants from a cake of soap (more suds, better fragrance, the fact it floats in the bathtub) and see if you want to change or modify the product in order to make the sale. You may decide too many changes are required and the potential buyer actually wants a bottle of perfume instead. So, no hard feelings. You'll take your soap else-where, to a place where they want soap, and may even buy your brand.

You may suspect this kind of analogy is useless because it sounds like a game and everybody knows LIFE is not a GAME. However, you should know interviewing IS a game, and the only way you can play is if you understand that. Learn the rules, abide by them and keep your feelings as separate as you can.

Second rule: *Understand the objectives of the interview.*

In order to determine what information about yourself is relevant, you must establish the objective of the interview.

If the object of a baseball game is to win and a team wins by getting more runs than the other team, the players must understand and take those actions likely to produce runs.

Knowledge of the objective produces legitimate actions geared to achieving that objective. This may sound stuffy but all it means is when you play tennis you bring along your tennis racket and leave your water wings at home. Understanding the objective leads to appropriate behavior.

As a rule, there are two participants in the interview: the interviewer (the buyer) and the interviewee (the seller). Occasionally there is more than one interviewer; that happens in a "group" interview, but is unusual and the same rules apply anyhow.

Each player has a different objective.

In a job interview, the interviewer's purpose is to evaluate the candidate and predict her job performance.

This should be his *only* objective. No matter what direction the conversation takes, no matter what chemistry takes place between the participants, this is the interviewer's objective.

Quite often you will run into an interviewer who does not understand what his objective is. Few people who are empowered to hire people are trained as interviewers, which is a shame because the proper techniques save a lot of time and heartache.

Don't be intimidated because you think the interviewer's role in the interview is more important than yours. Your role is as important as is his. He may or may not end up making a job offer. This is where he derives his importance. He probably wants you to succeed in the interview as much as you do. Put yourself in his shoes. He has a position he wants to fill. He may or may not have seen other applicants before you. He is not *effective* until he has selected the person to fill the job. Unless he is an executive recruiter or an employment manager he has not had much experience with interviewing. He may be as uncomfortable about the situation as you are. Whether that's true or not, and it's likely to be true nine times out of ten, *he wants you to succeed.*

When an interviewer takes too much time describing the job and selling it to you, you can begin to suspect something is awry. Of course he must describe the job to you, but his purpose is to evaluate you and predict your job performance. He can't do that if he's doing all the talking.

The interviewer must understand what the position's requirements are, what its first-year goals are, what personality characteristics are most appropriate to the work setting, what skills and experience are imperative on Day One and what can be learned later. (You have to know these things, too.) He must evaluate you with these guidelines in mind: If he's given you too many clues about the position, you will attempt to fit yourself into the picture he has painted. That makes his job doubly difficult because he must then rely almost entirely on his instincts. Although an expert interviewer must have acute perceptions and instincts, he cannot afford to rely on them to any great extent. That gets too close to guesswork. The person he is interviewing (you) must give him the information he requires to make an appropriate judgment. He must believe the information he receives and certainly, even though it is subjective and highly personal, your contribution will be honestly presented.

It behooves the interviewer to provide an environment encouraging this honesty. "Stress" interviews are worthless because they assault the interviewee with so many threats she feels she must protect herself, becomes defensive, self-protective and wary of opening up and being honest. This is disastrous, an infringement of the interview's purpose. People who give "stress" interviews don't know what their objective is. There are other, less painful ways to assess a person's ability to handle stress and tension.

All this serves to demonstrate the interviewer is no more sacrosanct than you are. You *must* understand his purpose in order to understand clearly your own participation.

You, the interview*ee* have two objectives.

The primary objective is to present yourself as a competent, intelligent person who has valuable skills.

It may surprise you to learn your primary goal in an interview is *not* a job offer. Strange as that may seem, an offer comes about only when the interviewer and the interviewee mutually meet their objectives. He must feel you can do the job he has in mind, that you are a "good fit." This will come about because you have met your objective, you have persuaded him you are competent and intelligent.

Your other objective is to find out if you want the job if it is offered.

Until you are an old hand at interviewing, you will occasionally slide into the comfortable pattern of trying to please the fellow across the desk. Pleasing him and making him feel good feels familiar, safe. It takes the form of reassuring him you like the job he's talking about (and by implication *him* since it is *his* job). If you're encouraging him to feel terrific about the position he is describing, you are not listening to see if it pleases you.

Meeting of the mutual objectives may take more than one meeting: an initial screening and evaluation and a second (in some cases, even a third) interview at which time both of you recognize the possibility of selection.

When you understand your objectives, you can plan the ways you will achieve them.

Third Rule: *Prepare yourself.*

If success is part of your game plan, preparation for the game must be your first priority. (You started your preparations when you defined your objectives.)

In an interview you are selling your skills. If your resumé is the result of solid thinking and careful introspection, you will be familiar with exactly what those skills are and how you can best present them. Every word of your resumé should be familiar to you.

Do your homework. Everybody talks about "doing your homework" in advance of a business meeting in which a presentation is planned, when a product is being considered for purchase. What exactly does it mean, "doing your homework"?

Homework enables competent participation in an upcoming activity.

Often in school, and later, in business meetings, the purpose of homework becomes confused and sometimes it turns out to be busywork. When you suspect what you are doing has no practical application, it may have become busywork. You can request, obtain and read as many annual reports as you wish, study listings in *The Wall Street Journal,* but if you don't know why you are doing it, you won't know what to look for. It will be Sanskrit to you, too much information to assimilate. It is like being given an assignment to learn the history of China by next Tuesday. Why? To what purpose? The human brain is a remarkable computer but if definition of purpose is not clear, even it will prove inadequate to the task.

Many career counselors advise obtaining annual reports and scrutinizing company listings in various cumbersome directories in preparation for interviews. I've never thought this serves any useful purpose whatever, *if* the only reason for doing it has to do with making a good impression on the interviewer. The interviewer will receive a good impression when you are confident, well organized and enthusiastic. He will be additionally impressed if you ask thoughtful questions, listen to his answers and respond to what he says after appropriate reflection.

In this instance, then, doing your homework refers to preparing yourself so you will present yourself as yourself: an intelligent, resourceful person. If it makes you feel more comfortable to read up on all aspects of a company—its products, its history, its corporate officers, its industry and competition—by all means, do it. It isn't necessary to the outcome of the interview. If you find the collection and analysis of all that information overwhelming, leave it alone. Many people are not born researchers, including most businessmen.

Don't let what the experts say scare you. What you must do is understand your product (your experience, your qualifications, your skills) and how you can best present it.

Fourth Rule: *You set the agenda.*

An agenda is a planned program of topics and/or events which take place within a specified time frame.

You can predict a job interview's agenda because you

know what the objectives are. Within a certain period of time (probably less than an hour), several specific topics must be covered.

INTERVIEWER	INTERVIEWEE
1. Description of the job.	1. Description of qualifications
2. Evaluation of potential job performance.	2. Evaluation of the position at issue.

Think carefully about all four areas. Decide what questions are necessary in order to explore them. Yes, these are the questions you will be asked, and which you will ask.

Don't be afraid the interviewer will label you "aggressive" if you know what you're doing and understand what's going on. Aggression carries within it a large dose of hostility, and knowing what your objectives are doesn't make you feel hostile, it makes you feel *confident*.

You may, on occasion, come across some poor soul who is lacking in confidence himself. Once, when I was participating in an interview, I said, "I'm good at what I do." The interviewer frowned at me and said, "You'll have to be careful of that aggression. . . . Men don't like aggressive women." What he meant, of course, was *he* felt threatened by a *confident* woman, which is too bad for him and undoubtedly set the seal on any possibility of my working in his organization. It bothered me for a while until I realized I was falling into the old social trap of trying to modify my feelings and my behavior in order to please or satisfy my idea of what somebody else (male authority) wanted.

Get out of his head. You don't know what he's thinking. You are not a mind reader and neither is he.

You can no longer afford the luxury of designing yourself to please someone else. You may feel desperate, even in despair. Maybe you need this job more than anything else in the world and you need it *now*. Whatever you do, don't fall into that "pick-me-and-I'm-yours" trap. It won't help you get a job. The only reason you consider it is its familiarity. The job marketplace is not the senior prom. You must appear competent and confident. If you are easily deflated and frantic to please, your insecurity will send messages no hiring manager can ignore. He will not want you.

Rule Five: *Never make demands in advance of a job offer.*

This should be obvious. It isn't. I have seen too many women fail initial interviews because they have told the interviewer they *have to* get home by 4:30 in the afternoon, *must* have four weeks' vacation so they can get away to the Islands with their families as they do every year. Your objective is to demonstrate competence and intelligence, not to finagle accommodation to your particular circumstances. When you receive a job offer, then you negotiate modifications.

Setting up a network of demands makes it that much easier for a potential employer to turn his back on you. "You know how housewives are," he will tell his (male) cohorts over their Perriers. "They can't work straight hours, one week after another, like other people. Their families and homes always interfere, always come first. It's a pity, but it's not my fault."

You are free to mediate changes in working hours or responsibilities *after* and *not before* the offer.

What Questions Will Be Asked?

The questions the interviewer will ask you will have to do with you. Your experience. Your skills. Your ability to assume specific responsibilities, to follow through. He wants to know about past performance. This throws light on future performance and helps him to predict it.

There are a hundred questions he may ask. They can be reduced to four general areas:

1. Where have you been?
2. Where are you now?
3. Where are you going?
4. How much money do you want?

Your answers can be prepared in advance.

Sometimes the interviewer will throw you a curve,

decidedly outside these four general areas, at least at first flush. He knows it's a trick and asks it mostly to see how well you can field the question or what kind of a person you are. Once I asked a fellow (a candidate for a pharmaceutical marketing job) if any book he had read had changed his life. (The question seems pretentious now.) His reply, "Yes, *The Last Temptation of Christ*," floored me and we went on to have a very enjoyable and, for me, enlightening conversation. Actually, the question wasn't so wild. It fell neatly into the "Where have you been?" category. I asked it because I wanted to learn the kind of imagination and intellect he possessed. These are important characteristics for a marketing professional. I certainly learned what I wanted.

In general, your product (you) has specific characteristics (skills/qualifications) you have identified and have decided will be part of your selling presentation. That's why introspection was a necessary ingredient of your resumé preparation. Since the resumé is the brochure for your product, the interview is complemented by the printed material.

Therefore, if you have decided a description of your communications skills should be a major portion of your resumé, you will design your answers in the interview using exactly the same technique you used when preparing your resumé:

Objective: Action Steps: Result

Just as this superstructure helped you organize the exposition in the resumé, so, too, will it help you sort out your thoughts and give you a framework for what you will say. No matter what you are asked, your answers will be orderly; there will be a beginning, a middle and an end, because you will be talking in paragraphs. You won't ramble and go off track. You will sound (because you *are*) well organized, thoughtful, prepared.

Here is a sample conversation using the material from one of the resumés included in Chapter 3 (p. 123):

INTERVIEWER
Tell me about yourself (where have you been?).

INTERVIEWEE
  During the past several years I've developed skills as a
  communicator and motivator. Which skill would you
  like me to describe?

  This may sound like the old door-to-door salesman
gimmick ("Which set of satin sheets are you going to order,
the red or the black?"), but don't be embarrassed about it.
You are not selling red satin bedsheets. You are selling a
valuable product—yourself—and if the technique is similar,
the products are not. The reason the technique is so
familiar is it works. You will feel self-conscious at first, but
when you see how easily the conversation goes, you will
relax. You may even learn to enjoy it.

INTERVIEWER
  Tell me about your communication skills.

INTERVIEWEE
  As Citizen Monitor for the Community Council of
  Greater New York, my charter was to evaluate the
  effectiveness of two federal government funded projects. As a volunteer I made formal and informal visits to
  the program offices and work sites to interview project
  leaders, their assistants and the participants, both in
  groups and individually. Since it was necessary to collect
  honest, uncensored information, particularly from program recipients, I often joined and worked along with
  the job teams, talking with them as we performed the
  tasks. At the conclusion of this evaluation process, I
  drafted a recommendation which included a summary of
  the objective of each program, an analysis of its leadership and activities, and a rating of its overall effectiveness and efficient use of funding. I evaluated approximately twenty programs in a fifteen-month period.

  Use the same or similar language you used on your
resumé. (Don't memorize it: Recitation gives your conversation a stilted, unnatural tone.) The interviewer may
have read your resumé, but he will not have *studied* it. Your
discussion will serve either to refresh his memory of your

experience and the skills you have to offer, or it will be new information to him. If that is the case, when he reads the resumé after you've left, your interview will serve to set the product in his mind, which is what a good brochure does. The resumé and the interview are closely connected, enhancing and complementing each other.

INTERVIEWER
What do you plan to be doing five years from now? (Where are you going?)

INTERVIEWEE
I see myself in an interesting management position using my training in Art History and the skills I have developed as a communicator and organizer.

As you can see, this response is cribbed directly from the *objective* on her resumé. It makes sense, doesn't it?

No matter what questions are asked, remember the primary objective. You are here to sell your skills, to demonstrate you are competent and intelligent. Every question the interviewer asks can be answered with that objective in mind.

Money Talks

There are at least two reasons an interviewer asks how much money you want.

1. To learn what you think your value is.
2. To see if you will remove yourself from his consideration by shooting too high or too low.

He has no need to ask for your help in determining possible salary. He doesn't need to know how much he should offer you. He knows that already. He knows approximately how much he is going to pay the person he hires to fill the position for which he's interviewing. He has a budget. Payroll is no mystery to him.

In the money department, his objective is to hire the best possible person for the lowest possible amount of money. Your objective is to get the maximum amount of money within the salary range which he knows about and you don't. This puts you at a disadvantage. All is not lost, however. Think about it this way: If you had been working steadily for many years, you would have some idea of the salary you could command (not necessarily what you would be worth) and you wouldn't be able to go much beyond that figure. Your reply to him would reflect this knowledge. Since you haven't been working for a paycheck, you don't know what the going rate is for the skills you are offering. Your answer, therefore, is appropriate to your situation:

> I'd rather not talk about money until we are discussing a specific job offer. When I can assess what my responsibilities will be, what the challenges are, the variables and the expectations you have, then I can talk sensibly. I'm reluctant now to go into it.

Sometimes the interviewer won't accept this answer and will press further. He will want to find out what you *think* you're worth—a "ball park figure."

There is no way to answer this question. As a housewife, you have received no salary, even though fifteen or twenty years of your life have gone into the vocation. How can you possibly determine what the going rate is for the skills you have developed as a housewife and volunteer? You gave these services away. There are no legitimate economic guidelines which might serve to offer clues.

Given your situation, this is not a valid question. Tell him so, firmly and pleasantly.

"Perhaps you can help me out by telling me the salary range for the position we're talking about." That puts the ball solidly back on his side of the net.

He must pay what the position is budgeted for, not what he thinks you will accept. Therefore, your opinion of your value is not helpful to him and he has no business asking you what you think you're worth or how much you need to live on. Those are not businesslike questions, if he is interviewing you for a specific position.

Remember there is no way for you to know the salary

he has in mind, unless he tells you what it is. The moment you tell him the absolute minimum figure you will accept, that's the offer he will make. He is not your best friend. He is a businessman. Any time you give a precise figure or talk about a three or four thousand dollar range ($12,000 to $15,000), he's got you on the low figure and that's what he will offer. Keep mum.

Pitfalls

Don't expect divine inspiration to rescue you and never, never lie. If you don't know something, say so. Lying gets you in terrible trouble—even little white lies (your age, for example). If you aren't found out at once, you will expect to be found out momentarily and will never stop looking over your shoulder.

One of the mistakes women make in interviews is to confess all. This comes about partly because of the Bene-factor-to-Supplicant aura I talked about earlier. It is tempting to tell everything (bare your soul) to the author-ity figure who is, after all, asking you questions about yourself and nodding sympathetically in response to your answers.

Beware! He is not interested in the fact your husband ran away with his secretary (twenty years younger than he) or your recent widowhood has left you with eleven dollars in the bank and a daughter at Dennison. He doesn't care about your feelings of uncertainty and insecurity, or what heartbreaking or trivial events have led you to his office. Why should he care?

Unless the information you are giving bears directly on the objective of the interview, keep it to yourself. No matter how much you yearn for sympathy and under-standing, for support, affirmation, encouragement, a job interview is not the place to look for it. *Keep your eye on the sparrow.* A job interview is a business meeting, not a therapy session, a consciousness raising or encounter group.

You are not making friends in an interview. For this reason you are careful to avoid any behavior suggesting the meeting is not pure business. Although men and women who have been working for years may enjoy the relaxed atmosphere of a job interview which takes place over lunch or drinks, you cannot. Having come so recently out of the kitchen, you cannot afford any activity suggesting you are naive or unfamiliar with standard business procedure.

If the person with whom you are meeting is an old friend, you may have to make an exception. But be prepared for the awkwardness when the check comes. You should probably let him pay, even though you invited him, *if he asks*. If he wants to have three martinis, you don't have to match him, drink for drink, even though you may feel judgmental and unpleasant when you nurse your single gin and tonic or Tab.

Don't permit the conversation to fall into the gentle, familiar, old-friend melody (telling about your children, asking about his, laughing about old times, telling jokes, being charming). Don't do that at all; or, if you must, only after you are satisfied the interview has ended. Anything interfering with his perceptions of you as a competent person should be avoided. And when you are laughing about last summer's clam bake when little Lucy fell into the river and had to be fished out with a butterfly net, he cannot possibly see you in an office environment. Be fair to him, and to yourself. The prejudices about you which he brings with him to the meeting must be laid aside. You must be perceived in a new light and you must help him do that.

One of the questions likely to be asked at a job interview has to do with your strengths and weaknesses. When you are in a confessional and somebody asks you to describe your weaknesses, you might be tempted to describe how you cry easily, react badly to criticism or drink too much when under pressure. *No good!*

Why would such honesty meet your objectives at the job interview? Don't be seduced by a relaxed atmosphere into making such damaging revelations. Your personal hangups are no business of your potential employer. Remember you are selling a product. The buyer will discover the warts and flaws after he has made his purchase. That's expected. Don't worry about it or feel guilty. In this game you are a salesman, so act accordingly.

Figure out something to say in response to the weakness question which will actually turn out to be a strength "I get impatient when people do less than they've promised." "I have a weakness for strong, clear declarative sentences." "I hate to be late." Since your reply is recognized as part of a sales technique, you don't have to worry about how deeply significant it sounds.

The only reason the interviewer has for asking the question is to spring a trap. You don't have to get angry about it (How dare he?), just recognize his purpose. How could you possibly answer this question honestly without damaging your case?

He knows that. Now you know it, too. You can manipulate the answer to your benefit. In tennis there is a time for an overhead smash and a time for a gentle lob. Consider this a gentle lob back to his court. You needn't be snide or defensive. Smile and relax. He'll get on with it when he sees that you understand.

Always Be Positive

I almost headed this section *Never Be Negative*, which goes to show doing as I say isn't always easy, even for me.

It takes a lot of practice in order to speak positively. Negative conversation is readily identified when you know what to listen for, even if it contains no negative words. It is whiney, full of excuses or self-justification, defensive. It uses words like "I only . . ." or "just because . . ." and connects clauses with "but" and is a bad sales technique.

I worked recently with two clients, both of whom were sixty years old. Jill T. was beautifully dressed, looked younger than her age (not as young as she imagined she looked, but younger than she was) and she sincerely believed her last responsible job had been with the Office of Price Administration during the Second World War. She refused to recognize she had done anything since 1945. "All I did was raise two children and run a household but my marriage turned out to be a failure (after thirty years!) I have done nothing in the last fifteen years and nobody wants to hear about it anyway." She got very angry with me when I could not give her a magic sentence to use in interviews which would make her age go away. She thought it was shameful to be sixty years old, hated being sixty years old and was certain everybody else felt the same way. What she really wanted to hear from me was that she was really forty-five years old; since I couldn't tell her that she exploded and stormed out of my office. I never saw her again.

Jane G. had graduated from college in 1939, raised two children and was a widow with a steadily decreasing income. She was sixty years old and looked seventy-five. What she had, however, which more glamourous Jill didn't, was enthusiasm and curiosity. How could she make her age an *advantage?* We were able to identify and describe the skills she had developed during thirty-five years of various types of distinguished volunteer service (she'd done her share of envelope licking as well as more visible organizing of committees and leading pickets at the state capital). She thought carefully about those job possibilities and areas where her age would be helpful to the performance of the tasks, and then she set out, by herself, in pursuit. Seven months later she was offered and accepted a job in a "senior citizen" center coordinating programs and obtaining speakers and teachers.

All a difference in attitude. Both women were self-conscious and embarrassed about how old they were, something they couldn't change. Jane, however, had a healthy attitude about it: There it is, it isn't going to go away, so what can be done with it? She turned her practical attention on her fear, and acted.

One of the lessons I keep learning and relearning is that everybody is frightened, shy, self-conscious and sure only of their inability to measure up.

I remember a section of Agatha Christie's memorable book, *An Autobiography* (Dodd, Mead), which applies here. Christie's books are, of course, read on several continents by millions of people. Her name is as close to being a household word as is that of any other twentieth-century author. But listen to her describe how she feels at a party *given in her honor* for the tenth anniversary of the continuous run of her play, *The Mousetrap*, in London:

* * *

. . . when I tried to enter the private room reserved for the party, I was turned back. "No admission yet, madam. Another twenty minutes before anyone is allowed to go in." I retreated. Why I couldn't say outright, "I am Mrs. Christie and I have been told to go in," I don't know. . . .

I suppose actually, the feeling is—I don't know whether every author feels it, but I think quite a lot do—that I am pretending to be something I am not, because, even nowadays, I do not quite feel as though I am an author. I still have that overlag of feeling that I am *pretending* to be an author. Perhaps I am a little like my grandson, young Mathew, at two years old, coming down the stairs and reassuring himself by saying,"*This is Mathew coming downstairs!*" And so I got to the Savoy and said to myself: "This is Agatha pretending to be a successful author, going to her own large party, having to look as though she is someone, having to make a speech that she can't make, having to be something that she's no good at."

I think every woman who reads this anecdote understands what Christie is talking about. We are all of us more alike one another than we are different from each other, rich and famous or no.

Remember Christie's story when you have an interview. Sail in, act *as if* you are confident and enjoying yourself. Soon you will be.

What To Do When the Offer Comes

Sooner or later, someone is going to offer you a job. He will describe its responsibilities and explain where the position fits into the corporate matrix. He will tell you what the salary is, some of the company benefits programs and, in fact, may do some selling of his own because, wonder of wonders, he has decided you are a person who will make a valuable employee.

If you have been waging a full-time job campaign, you will probably have other promising situations simmering offstage. I usually recommend you don't accept the first job offer that comes along. There are several reasons for this. Sometimes you aren't locked into a smooth and unhurried interview technique when the first offer comes, and you are tempted to take anything offered, even when it is clearly inappropriate. You think you can't last out the campaign, nothing else will come your way—the good old bird in the hand.

If the offer comes so early in your job campaign you haven't yet talked to several people and fairly assessed your own value, then you will be left with an incomplete, unfinished sensation, if you accept the job. You'll always wonder if you should have continued your search, if you would have benefited.

In addition, the first job offer almost never comes with anywhere near the salary you want. That's important, because every raise you get, every other job you ever interview for will be based on the salary you accept with your first, reentering job.

While I don't think you should take the first offer tendered, I know, too, we're only human. If you want it, take it. Do yourself a favor, though. Never accept a job on the spot. Bite your tongue. Tell your potential employer you need time to think it over. Then take some time. The offer won't go away, once it's been tendered. The person who makes you the offer will permit you time to reflect— often as much as two or three weeks. In that amount of time you can continue pursuing your other leads and thinking it over, just as you tell him you plan to do. After a suitable time has elapsed, then let him know your decision. If your answer to him is positive, you and he both will know you gave it thoughtful consideration before you accepted the offer.

That will do you both good.

Have a Good Time

The two most important elements for you in an interview are personal energy and confidence. Energy doesn't mean you leap around and laugh too loudly and shake hands like a stevedore; energy means there is breath supporting your voice so that it projects without jarring; energy means you make eye contact with the person across the desk, instead of looking timidly into your lap; energy sits up straight (not tensely, on the edge of the chair, or huddling into it); energy doesn't whine or have sick headaches.

Confidence comes when you know what you're doing. You're going to be meeting new people, talking about interesting things, observing, participating, learning.

Think of the process as an adventure, not an ordeal. Your world will enlarge in direct relation to the number and types of the people you meet and talk with at interviews.

Your apprehension is to be expected. You're putting yourself "on the line," and that means you're out there all alone.

Think of the payoff. It's worth it.

CHAPTER SIX

Afterwards

Demons That Come in the Night

What if you've gotten through all this material, have completed your *ideal job description*, written your *resumé*, planned and organized your job campaign and still harbor a persistent sinking feeling that working in an office is not what you were cut out for? Perhaps you have begun to suspect with increasing certainty the idea of reporting in at eight-thirty or nine in the morning and working steadily until five-thirty or so is not such a hot idea. Possibly you think you have pictured yourself in an office because that's the acceptable, available alternative. You're afraid you really hate the idea but don't have the imagination to think of something else.

Let's sort out some of these quandaries.

One possibility for your uneasiness may be your fear you won't fit in. You don't know what will be expected of you, whether anybody will like you, if you will be regarded as an old lady or an antediluvian example of the extinct species *housewife*. Will everyone be generations younger than you, brighter, more sophisticated?

These are expected insomnia-producing demons, satisfactorily laid aside two weeks after you start your new job.

People at the office, as well as elsewhere, come in all sizes and shapes, ages and I.Q's. As you get to know the people there and as they get to know you, differences erode and you fit in easily. You won't be any more or less peculiar and unusual than anybody else. You won't be the new kid for long. Fear of awful differences in age and general levels of greenness can be bracketed under fear of the unknown, and you know how to handle that by now.

What is more important, if you have created and developed your job campaign, if you understand the purpose of this scrutiny of your skills and motives, if you understand as well the actions and the reasons for the actions you take to reach your objective (a job offer), then your knowledge of what really goes on in an office—*any* office—is acute. Defining objectives, developing and implementing the actions leading to these objectives are crucial skills anywhere, especially in the office.

You don't lack understanding of goal setting and effective methodology (actions designed to achieve goals). This *modus operandi* is precisely what you learn as you design and implement your job campaign. You have taken every step yourself, so you intimately understand the process. Your job campaign is a microcosm of the business world itself. It was designed so the actions within it parallel actions taken within the business world. Your job campaign has helped to prepare you for your career in business, just as the experiences you've had in your lifetime have helped to make you mature, thoughtful and an asset to any *management by objective* program you encounter or help to design.

Lay the worry about being hopelessly unsophisticated and outclassed aside, too. You're not. Since you haven't worked in an office setting for a long time, the panic stemming from ignorance of procedure may be the main thing bothering you. You don't want to make silly mistakes because you're rusty or out of practice. You're agonizingly self-conscious.

Let's talk about what goes on inside those great gray walls. This will help ease your panic.

Settling In

No matter where you work, whether it is a big office or a small one, part of a large company or a little one, several basic characteristics of office life are always present.

1. *There is always someone to whom you report.* This means whatever it is you do must be delivered, in one way or another, to someone who has the authority to judge it. He can make you do it again, he can tell you it's a terrific piece of work or a failure; he has the right to say nothing at all about it. You will be operating under the umbrella of his personal style and idiosyncracies, intelligence and sets of priorities. You will be dependent on his good will. For that reason, when you interview for a job in an office, you must see if you can determine whether your proposed immediate superior is someone who is fair-minded. Of course there is no way you can make an unfailingly accurate judgment of his fair-mindedness in advance of working for him. But you should know it will be important to you as an employee. If he behaves unfairly in front of you before you accept the job (when he ought to be on his best behavior), be warned. It could be something in his attitude toward his secretary and the coffee pot or who is supposed to take your coat or return it to you, something quite minor. Watch for clues. Simply because the fellow is a male chauvinist (most middle-aged businessmen are) doesn't mean he is innately unfair about other things, such as job performance and recognition for a job well done, although blatant sexism ought to give you some fairly good clues about general mind-set and outlook. Mean-spirited people should be scrupulously avoided.

You must make sure you and your employer mutually understand the objectives for your position, both short and long range. Both of you must share the same understanding of your responsibilities. In order to achieve this understanding, you will ask questions when there is anything murky or in conflict with what you've been told before or what you understand to be the case.

Some people do not like working for other people. In some instances, this reluctance comes about because of a discomfort with authority or with the idea somebody else has veto power over their actions. On occasion, people (especially "loners") greatly dislike the lack of privacy in boss-employee relationships. They feel uncomfortable with the idea the boss can look over their shoulders, scan material before it's ready, ask them without warning about what they are planning to do this week on such and such a project. People like this resent filling out time sheets, punching time clocks and answering in other, more subtle ways, for the way they spend their time. If you are somebody like that, working in an office may not be a good idea for you. Analyze and understand the depth of the feeling. Nobody *likes* any of these things, they are irritants to the most relaxed and easygoing people among us. If, however, your distaste borders around the pathological fringes of outrage, you should be chary indeed about working in an office.

2. *There will be other people working around you.* You cannot control the selection of these other people. There is no way to tell in advance whether you will like them or not, whether you will be compatible with them, share mutual interests, whether you will be bored with or stimulated by the companionship of one another. Understand they will be important to you several hours every day, even if their responsibilities differ greatly from yours.

One of the difficulties experienced by a mature woman in a new management job, particularly when she has not worked for pay in several years, has to do with her social positioning in the office. Often the other females are clerks, typists, secretaries. The management people, the bosses or the ones next up the ladder are almost always male. The quandary is a simple one: With whom does one fraternize? Will you look like a snob or betrayer of your sex if you lunch only with the men? Men who are interested in moving ahead in firms rarely lunch on a regular basis with the secretaries, even their own secretaries, unless it's somebody's birthday or going away party or they are In Love (which happens). They go out with the other men or by themselves. It never occurs to them to do otherwise. They are men, after all, and, more important, at the office they are in a different working class from the women. They stick to their own kind. Should you?

There are a couple of angles to consider. Sometimes the question solves itself because of the nature of the woman involved. She comes in at a level below the department manager and his subordinate managers (all male) but above the other women. She feels most comfortable talking with the men in the office who are doing work similar to hers. So she socializes with them: She goes to lunch with them and sometimes (not often) goes to a local watering hole for a drink after work. She is not being flirtatious or looking for a husband; she finds, besides a conversational affinity with "the guys," she wants to be bracketed with the managers rather than with the managed. She doesn't relate particularly to the other women in the office, so she doesn't mix with them. In her case it is the sensible thing to do.

Many times well-brought-up women will call this *social climbing*. It is not. It is *working-class climbing*, and is always a characteristic behavior of upwardly mobile, ambitious employees. Knowledge of what *nice* people do and the fear of what they are going to say about what you do has prevented a lot of necessary speaking up and has permitted whole generations and types of people to be kept in their places. When we women in Pleasantville criticized feminists because we believed they were being shrill and unladylike, we never supposed they were fighting our battles. The truth is we criticized feminists because their outrage made us feel uncomfortable, made us question our choices, not because their voices were shrill. We characterized them that way because *nice* women have always kept their mouths shut while serving up the scrambled eggs.

Men on the rise have always acted on their ambition. Nobody calls them social climbers or makes them feel guilty because they want to get ahead.

If our ambitious businesswoman feels it makes more sense to deal habitually with the people whose levels of responsibility are similar to her own or slightly higher, that makes her sensible, not evil. Questions of "unsexing" oneself are not legitimate, either. Such questions throw sand in the face of common sense.

Another side of this baffling problem is, of course, many of the women who are roughly the same age, but not the same organizational level, may have similar interests outside the office. Also—and this is particularly true with women who are over forty years of age—the women in the office (clerks and secretaries) who are your age may have come from similar backgrounds to yours. Their education, their early lives, the books they read and even their politics may be like yours. Their children may be like yours, complete with the problems arriving automatically with adolescence. These woman may seem the kind of people with whom you once would have made friends because many of the things they talk about and think about are what interest you. The big difference between you and them may be you stayed home to raise your family and they went off to work. You may feel more comfortable with them, feel a greater sense of camaraderie, rapport and attraction than you do with the men or with the other managers.

Will fraternization with subordinate women damage your reputation and chances for advancement? Will it identify you with the *losers?* The answer depends on you. If any particular behavior causes you pain and embarrassment, jettison it. Acting against your instincts causes a breakdown in your set of values. When that happens, your behavior is uncertain, inconsistent. People who are unsure of what they are doing lack confidence. Nothing erodes confidence more quickly than behaving in ways you disapprove of. It's best to do those things which you feel most comfortable doing as long as no one is hurt, nobody's freedom is impinged. This leaves your personal integrity intact. If you are by nature a decent person, you will behave decently in most situations. You can count on it. By the time you are forty years old, you can trust yourself. Awareness of one's basic decency is one of the dividends of middle-age. Go to lunch with whomever you wish.

3. *Time is of the essence.* When you work in an office, your time is not your own, except on weekends, early in the morning, in the evening and during lunch. This means many of the chores you would ordinarily perform will no longer get done. Comparison shopping wastes time because it means you have to go to several stores before you make a purchase. Time, as a commodity, is too precious for the office worker to squander. No third cups of coffee at

the kitchen table over the crossword puzzle. If you plan to shop during your lunch hour, know everyone else in town has the same idea, so it will take three times as long as it usually does. Taking your lunch hour late, say, between three and four o'clock, is frowned on by most bosses because they are back from their lunches by then and not normally flexible enough to be able to handle an empty desk at unconventional hours. They feel taken advantage of.

Probably you can't get your hair done in an hour, so you will have to use some of your precious Saturday time for that unless you can find a hairdresser who stays open evenings. Most service transactions are run on a nine to six basis (although many stores blessedly remain open Thursday nights). Doctor appointments, dentist dates, driving lessons, television and other appliance repair must all be accommodated during the work week at the convenience of the person providing the "service." Few of these people work on weekends. All of the activities in which your children are involved have to accommodate your schedule now, too. You will feel guilty if you take time from your salaried job to do the family things you once did, so understand even if the boss and the workplace seem amenable to your taking time off for family crises, you won't want to do it often.

4. *What to wear?* You may be worried about what you're supposed to wear, especially if you've been wearing jeans (not the designer kind) for the last seventeen years. Women's magazines are invariably full of articles about just such matters. Photographs of twenty-eight-year-old models in Christian Dior outfits tend to put you off when your daily wardrobe decision centers on the choice between the sweatshirt with the egg stain or the sweater with the holes in the elbows. Women in Christian Dior outfits used to look like pod people to me and it was beyond my grasp and capacity to contemplate what the stylish professional women were wearing.

Then I read that book which told about how women were supposed to dress if they wanted to look successful (*looking* successful being the first step toward *being* successful, an intelligent, if unprofound observation). To my relief, I learned, once again, "experts" don't always know what they're talking about.

The author of the book had evidently questioned male business executives to see what "look" signaled prosperity and professionalism in a female worker. The businessmen were given photographs of women wearing various out-fits—a blouse and a skirt, a suit with a skirt, a suit with pants, a dress, etc. The majority of these important men classified the women who wore a blouse and skirt as a "secretary." The book's author took this to mean a woman who wanted to get ahead should never wear a blouse and skirt because it categorized her in a negative way. I was not impressed with his reasoning. I did not know who these businessmen were or what companies they worked in, but I imagined whoever they were, wherever they were, the only women who worked around them *were* secretaries. Moreover, most women who wear suits to the office (high on the list of desirability) take off the jacket sometime during the day (like the moment they get to work) and can a man tell if a blouse and skirt is actually that or a suit with its jacket elsewhere? (I can't.) The same holds for a blazer, blouse and skirt combination, which seemed to be the prize-winning outfit.

The book was widely read and accepted; there was a period of about two years when every secretary in New York City wore a straight skirt, a turtleneck sweater and a blazer. (It became the uniform of the upward-aspiring female functionary.) All because of this man's peculiar assumption a wardrobe can be determined by majority vote and successful men know best what successful women should wear.

Thank heavens for common sense. You have to wear what you think is appropriate and what you feel is comfortable.

By this time in your life, you have achieved your own personal style, reflected in the way you dress. You may not be aware of it and may not even be able to describe what it is. If that is the case, ask your family to help you. Show them a fashion magazine and ask them to pick out the Mom clothes. You will be able then to ascertain the kinds of clothes other people think of as what you select and wear. That is your personal style. You may be surprised. If the image of yourself you have been creating is one you don't particularly want to perpetuate, change it. Decide how you want to look and then, whenever you go clothes shopping, purchase those items which dovetail neatly with the minds' eye picture of yourself you are designing.

What you don't want to do is dress like you're "supposed" to dress. When you do that, you are being dressed by Them, somebody else who isn't you. I'm not recommending you dress in an outlandish or inappropriate manner, only that you decide for yourself how you like to look and what you like to wear. Responsibility for oneself begins when you choose your clothes.

I was reading a business magazine not long ago and saw a photograph which amused me. It pictured the board of directors of some gigantic multinational oil company getting off a plane. They were all smiling and talking comfortably to one another as people do who are doing what they like to do. The striking thing about the photograph was everybody in it looked exactly the same! Each dark suit was three-piece, beautifully tailored and exactly one inch too short in the pants, revealing too much dark socked ankle on all five men. The haircuts were all identical (one man was bald—I think he was the flamboyant one, the one who was president of a consumer goods company instead of a banker, as everyone else seemed to be). The reason businessmen dress alike is corporations are structured on the military model and uniforms are one of the ways in which rank is signified. If you, as a lowly corporal, dress like the general, someone may think you *are* the general. Even if that doesn't happen, you are demonstrating you know how to be a general because you know how to look like one.

There is no way women can look exactly like men, even if we wear pin-striped pantsuits and neckties. We have hips and bosoms and men don't and that's the way it is. As more and more women are accepted in management circles, the dress code will break down. Women will bring flair and color to corporate board-rooms. Someday men will laugh with disbelief when they are told they used to dress in uniforms to go to work. Women's liberation frees both sexes, you know.

A man told me once he had read a book about clothes for business men (I wondered what it could have talked about for 250 pages) and one of the things the author stressed was "no man who is serious about getting ahead in business would ever wear a brown suit." My reaction to this statement pretty much sums up my feeling about worrying over what to wear. I think the statement is pretentious, intolerant and hilarious. When common sense is forgotten, people can make the most preposterous statements and other people will nod and agree.

You have to use your sense of what is practical, becoming and appropriate. Nobody else can do this for you. Remember style has nothing to do with fashion or fads, convention or noncomformance. Style is your personal message to the world and nobody except you can write it.

Probably the basic rule about clothes is *simplicity is elegance.* Katharine Hepburn and Lauren Bacall will be remembered long after Twiggy or the cover girl in purple harem bloomers have been forgotten. Classics last.

5. *Offices are often fraught with intrigue.* People in offices, being human, often do foolish and/or harmful things to one another and sometimes they are self-destructive.

In offices of more than two people, there are usually two pecking orders: The first comes about as a function of authority, or the hierarchial nature of the office structure reproduced on the organizational chart in the boss's desk drawer; the second has to do with political influence. The people who can influence authority (even if their jobs seem to be minor) are important to the way things are run—*and to the relative safety, potential and importance of your job.* You have to keep your eye out to see where the political power lies. Sometimes it resides within the person of the boss's secretary (not always), sometimes a trusted assistant who may be way down on the management ladder. The structure of political power does not run parallel to the lines of authority; it is convoluted, capricious. It has more to do with who has the ear of authority and who knows best how to manipulate the decision-making people. These issues are sometimes difficult to determine.

Occasionally, you will come across an office where Sex has reared its toothsome head. If you find yourself in such an office, get out as fast as you can. It's no joke. All rules are suspended: All is lost.

Of all the different office interpersonal relationships, illicit sexual ones (they are always illicit, always "secret") are the worst.

I'm not against sex. I think hugging and kissing and concomitant delights are great. However, at The Office it is TROUBLE. Unless the people involved have jobs in different departments altogether, or work at *exactly* the same level with totally different responsibilities in the same department, there is no way good will come of it.

Consider the following chart:

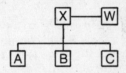

In this illustration, W is X's secretary. You can see A, B and C each report directly to X. Whatever their titles and functions, A, B and C are equal to each other in rank. In the usual business situation, while W, as a secretary, may be privy to many of the management problems and decisions faced by X, she is in a position to do nothing but carry out his instructions. Certainly, if X and W have a good working relationship, and if X respects W's intelligence and business savvy, she may be asked to give her opinions in specific matters. If she thinks her boss is a dud, she will keep her mouth shut and follow his orders anyway. If he thinks she is a dimwit, he won't consult with her, even informally. No matter how terrific or non-terrific she is as a human being and as a woman, the secretary's function in the office is clerical and she and her boss never forget it.

The responsiblities A, B and C have are not affected by the relationship between X and W *under ordinary circumstances.*

When X and W are having a love affair, however, all bets are off. X and W always think it is the first time it has ever happened to anyone (lovers are like that), they will be able to keep it under control, nobody will ever catch on and it will affect no one else. That's why Sex-in-The-Office is always kept secret from the beginning, even if neither person is married, if one participant works *for* the other. The intent of the secrecy is to keep everything under control, to act as if life is exactly as before the thunderclap. This is impossible.

Sooner or later, W will say to X (this is pillow talk and there's no way to protect yourself from it), "If you love me, you will give me more responsibility at the office." Or X will say to W, "Because you are in a better position to know than I am, and because everybody likes and trusts you (not always true, especially after a few months of The Affair), I want you to help me by being my eyes and ears and telling me what is going on in the office, no matter how unimportant."

Several things happen under these circumstances. The secretary begins to receive assignments which ordinarily and legitimately reside with A, B or C. Unrest, jealousy, resentment and rebellion flourish among the troops. W wasn't hired to do these things and often she is not capable of doing them. Secretaries are not trained to be managers. A, B and C aren't sure *what* W is doing; nobody tells them and they become paranoid.

In addition, A, B and C soon become aware they are being spied upon by the boss's secretary and at different times their responses will be to tell W nothing and to gradually put distance between themselves and her. Often A, B and C will tell W what they want the boss to think, whether it is true or not.

It is ludicrous to presume the situation will remain "secret." The troops will complain to one another but withhold trust from each other because they won't be able to decide if anybody else has W's special attention. Each will try separately to curry W's attention. Everybody will undercut the other guy. All such behavior is disastrous for the office.

The problem becomes exacerbated when the chart changes to:

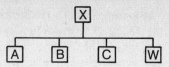

because even if the organization chart is drawn in this way, actually it has become the "Hanging W":

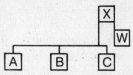

There is no way A, B and C can remain competent and well motivated because each of them knows their responsibilities may be altered, changed or eliminated at any moment, arbitrarily. They are helpless to do anything about it. Moreover, W's responsibilities will be amorphous, undefinable, always shifting and uncertain because she works at the whim and fancy of her boss and sometimes she won't be able to do the things she does well because he will want her to do something else. Her objective will have changed to one in which she must please him and that's not necessarily the same thing as doing a good job.

Pep talks from the boss, raises, staff meetings—nothing can change a situation like this, clearly in a state of progressive decay. The problem *cannot be solved*. No one is allowed to talk about it to the people who are involved, so it can only get worse. Because communication between the various managers and department functionaries is essential to effective office business behavior, management can no longer be effective. Good-bye efficiency, good-bye morale, good-bye employees, good-bye profit. Good-bye.

If you are tempted to become a W or an X, *resist it*. Critical judgment faculties are the first casualties in an office romance. No matter how sensible you and your *objet d'amour* are ordinarily, neither of you will be able to maintain equilibrium. If you can't resist the temptation, you or he must leave immediately and go elsewhere (you can continue the relationship at long distance, if you so choose). There is no other way to handle it. You have to make sure your exit is dignified and not propelled by circumstances making you look ridiculous, so you don't want to be forced out. Given the way things are in society nowadays, the one to leave is almost always the woman. She is usually forced to leave and businessmen really close ranks against her. If you think being forced out is acceptable after all the agony and hard work you went through to get the job in the first place, consider victims of injustice rarely get a second chance. Once set on course, there is no way back.

If you like your job, hang in there. Do *not* succumb. This, too will pass (unromantic, but, alas, true) and you will be proud of your strength.

Other Worries

Some difficulties are peculiarly characteristic of re-entering women with families. Questions occurring with regularity include:

What am I going to do with the kids?

How am I going to manage to get dinner on the table every night?

When will the chores get done?

Will they get done?

What will happen to the comfortable (or uncomfortable) life-style in my home when I am no longer there to supervise what goes on?

Your first line of information, as always, is your friends and acquaintances. They are your allies. One woman is not able to solve successfully the new and unfamiliar difficulties when she is faced with the thousand responsibilities and requirements springing up when she returns to the paid work force. She and others like her must learn the lessons other working people have learned: organization. When people with similar goals and requirements band together it is far more likely objectives will be achieved. Take your problems seriously (they are not unique; you are not at fault). Call up your working-mother friends, as well as others who, like you, are starting to look for new jobs. Try to meet with them and their friends, ideally on a regular basis. Share your ideas, your problems. Brainstorm in those areas where the contribution of more than one point of view is likely to be helpful. Find out what the others plan to do with their children or what they have done, how they get them to and fro, for example, what baby-sitters they use, if there is a local agency or clearing house for information about sitters or day-care centers. If your children are infants or preschoolers, the issue of day-care centers immediately comes to mind.

In addition to your friends, people at a local school or church should know where your town's day-care centers are located. If they don't, other working mothers will. Speak to your pediatrician, or his nurse or his receptionist. What do they do with their children? What do their daughters do with theirs? If all else fails, when no word-of-mouth seems available, get out your dependable telephone book. Look up the listings under U.S. Government in the white pages. Depending on the size of your community, you will find a federal information-center telephone number you can call to ask questions if you can't find another suitable place. Other useful federal government listings include your congressman's office, the Community Services Administration, the Department of Education (which supervises educational programs like Head Start and other national attenders to children's needs), the Department of Health and Human Services (their Children's Bureau), the Department of Labor, which has a Women's Bureau. Your state government listings may include listings for your state legislator's office, the state's Education Department, its Labor Department, Department of Social Services (this will include services for children). If your city is large enough, relevant listings include the various schools and the Board of Education, the Agency for Child Development or Children's Services, or Resource Centers, the Mayor's office, the city's Department of Social Services, if any. Many of these places may be able to answer the questions you have or will be able to refer you to places whose spokespeople can. Remember that elected officials are there to serve and represent you. Don't be afraid you're being pushy. Helping you to address these problems is precisely what they're supposed to be doing, and they have, as they should, great amounts of information and knowledge about these matters. Never be afraid to ask.

When you home in on a day-care center, remember it is a place to take care of your children, and the mere fact of its existence doesn't mean you have achieved Nirvana. You must be persuaded it is the right and proper place for your offspring. Sample questions you will want to ask include:

Are there licensing requirements for day-care centers in our community?

If so, what are they?

What body or agency is in charge of the licensing procedures? (That's the place which will have lists of all appropriately licensed facilities.)

If not, is there any criteria or uniform standards applied to day-care centers by any governmental or other body?

When there is no firm licensing requirement, you must become your own licensor. You will want to know about the following important aspects of the day-care centers:

What is the ratio of the number of children to supervising adults? (An adult is over eighteen.)

What is the age, condition, types of play equipment, both indoors and outdoors?

What are the activities, programs, schedules?

Is there a piano, a record player, books?

What are the meal and snack provisions?

How much does it cost?

What kind of financial assistance is available to parents who need it?

What are the hours?

Write down the questions you intend to ask before you get on the telephone. You will find that prevents your hanging up before you've found out all you want to know. Take notes, too. Often we don't remember precisely what people say, and in this instance, when you will be talking to more than one person, it is important afterwards to have a method of sorting out the information different people give you. Remember, too, it is their answers that must please and satisfy you—and not the other way around.

Other areas to which you will want specific answers have to do with questions of costs other than tuition (mysterious or straightforward extra fees, transportation costs, food costs, if any), acceptance criteria and average ages of children in the center, length of time it has been operating, background of principle supervisors, transportation provisions, if any, other parents and their addresses and telephone numbers. Make sure you understand everything. If you don't, keep asking until you do.

If you live in a community where no facilities are available to care for the children of working parents, the working parents themselves must solve the matter. Often they band together to form day-care cooperatives, or petition a large employer of working parents in their community (through unions or schools or in an organized parent association of some kind) to provide services for the very young children of their employees.

Two divorced women I know who needed to return to paid work had a total of six children under the age of eight. Instead of wailing and bemoaning their unlucky fates, these spunky women formed a "childhood center" in conjunction with a local church which quickly became a paying proposition. It answered a vital community need, identification of which is one of the first ways to determine what business venture is likely to succeed. They were able to kill two birds with one stone by focusing on their own needs and simultaneously accommodating their neighbors.

Other possibilities which warrant examination have to do with *flex-time* (jobs during other hours than nine to five, Monday through Friday, thus enabling you to arrange child-care chores with your husband, other family members or neighbors, unavailable at usual times), part-time or shared jobs. When you share a job (sometimes called *team* jobs) with another woman with children, you take care of the combined offspring while she's at work, she cares for them while you're at work. Such an accommodation often makes up for the smaller pay check since child-care costs don't have to be subtracted.

Here is a further sampling of resources in this general field:

The Day Care and Child Development Council of America, 1520 Southern Building, 805 Fifteenth Street, NW, Washington, D.C. 20005, functions as a national information center about child-directed services and offers advice about program planning, fund raising and organizational techniques. Its objective is "the creation in every community of a comprehensive system of daytime service aimed at helping children develop their full human potential—intellectually, physically, emotionally and socially."

The National Black Child Development Institute, 1463 Rhode Island Avenue, NW, Washington, D.C. 10005, was founded in 1970 and endeavors to develop quality child-centered programs buttressed by community and economic development. It distributes information on federal and state programs.

The National Association for Child Development and Education, 1800 M Street, NW, Washington, D.C. 20036, has fifteen hundred members representing privately owned child-care centers in ten state groups.

The Children's Foundation, 1420 New York Avenue, NW, Suite 1112, Washington, D.C. 20036, is a nonprofit advocacy organization focusing on federal food assistance programs for needy children and their families. The group publishes *The Family Day Care Bulletin* as well as a Directory of Special Supplemental Food Programs for Women, Infants and Children. The Directory includes approximately fifteen hundred local, state and Department of Agriculture programs, including county maps. It cost $2.50 in 1979.

If yours are older elementary-school aged children, the hours between three o'clock and five-thirty (whenever you or your husband get home) are crucial.

Too old to qualify for preschool all-day care programs, too young to care for themselves, especially in cases of emergency, this is a particularly knotty age. Sometimes day-care centers have provisions for older children. Sometimes baby-sitters can be arranged for, either on an individual family basis or when two or three families pool their children and their resources. Pooling needs and resources is a good solution when the high school cheer-leader baby-sitter is unavailable or there is no Aunt Minnie or Grandma available to watch the kids and to bake cookies on wintery afternoons. Again, the way to find out who the others are who need the same kind of help as you do is to ask. Speak to your children's teachers. They know other mothers. They can provide you with the names, addresses and phone numbers of other parents in the class. Think of the school as the center of child-centered activities and the basic source of help in this area. Sometimes after-school programs can be arranged at the schoolhouse itself if there are enough parents who are willing to arrange it and to participate.

You may be flabbergasted when you discover the spirit of neighborliness and cooperation that lurks, often un-tapped, under the surface of your community—even if it is a crowded urban one, even if it is a rural area where houses are miles apart.

Another source to look into is the American Home Economics Association which espouses "survival skills" for what are often referred to as "latchkey" children: children of parents who both work away from home. The practical courses they offer include cooking real meals, taking care of clothes (washing and simple repairs), planning meals and purchasing foodstuffs, basic nutrition and infant-care. These courses are taught in public schools all over the country, including elementary schools, and they are taught to boys *and* girls. What a boon. This Washington, D.C.-based national organization (address: 2010 Massachusetts Avenue, NW, Washington 10036) has an office in every state, usually in the state capitol, and is an excellent source of information about family help programs. Future Home-makers of America addresses itself to concerns of modern parents and children. This group is a unit of the American Home Economics Society, and is headquartered at the same Washington, D.C. address.

The Girls Clubs of America and the Girl Scouts have national headquarters and state offices and people in them who devote time to dealing with the problems of school age children whose parents work.

There is a whole raft of jobs mothers have traditionally done for their children: Brownie and Girl Scout leader, den mother, class mother. You may feel a sense of obligation to fulfill some or one of these functions despite the difficulty of fitting it around your schedule. It is important for you to know your children do not feel deprived.

When my children were in elementary school, and although I wasn't working at a job yet, I was going to school four out of five weekdays, I was a class mother for at least one year for each of my children, for no good reason except I wanted to feel I was doing my duty. It wasn't such a big deal, being a class mother. It required phoning other parents to tell "no school" on snow days (and being phoned myself with the good news by some school person at the customary 5:30 A.M. total blackness), providing cookies and milk on mornings of class party days and being there on Open House nights to help out the teacher by providing cute little name tags ("Hello! My name is . . ."). All of these things could have been done even if I had been commuting to a paid job in a distant city. You don't have to give up being class mother if you're working at a paid job. You may not want to be class mother and are looking for a legitimate excuse to avoid the task. That's another issue and I suggest you face it squarely. Discuss it with your family. They will understand. Everybody, even very young persons, knows about feeling pressured to fulfill hated obligations. You don't want to blame your job for everything unpleasant happening in your life. Then *Mom's job* will become a scapegoat. Everybody will feel neglected and/or unfairly treated and it will always be your fault. If you don't want to be class mother, say so. Be honest, then nobody will feel guilty.

Being a den mother or a Girl Scout or Brownie leader may be more difficult to arrange even if you want to do it, if you're working at a five-day-a-week paid job. Cubs, Brownies and Girl Scouts usually meet on a regular afternoon every week. Often the meeting dates and times are inflexible because there are other mothers involved and changes bring on chaos. The way they rope you into this kind of service is through use of the device of a last-minute, very-late-at-night phone call (usually the caller is some poor tired soul who has been working too many years at running a Cub Scout pack and feels nobody appreciates her considerable effort, especially her own children who *hate* being Cubs) telling you, "It looks like poor little Geoffrey and his friends won't be able to be Cub Scouts because nobody is willing to take the trouble to become den mother." That sentence is geared to bring even the most recalcitrant among us to our knees and is probably why the Scout movement continues to flourish in the United States. When that argument was used on me when Tom was eight, I didn't bite but David did and he became den mother to five little boys (including Tom) who came joyously to our house very Saturday morning, burst in the front door in their clean blue and yellow uniforms, bolted down the hall and out the back door for a fine game of football in which their uniforms became suitably mud-caked and torn every week. Our boys may not have been able to tie creditable knots in campers' competitions or to recite various pledges and creeds at the annual Blue and Gold dinner, but they all knew a forward from a lateral pass and each of them loved "scouting." I think dads who become den mothers have a fine time and I think it is not beneath them to become Brownie or Girl Scout leaders either. If women can be den mothers to little boys, men can be Brownie leaders to little girls. Why not? They've been Boy Scout leaders for generations and meeting times and other details have always been arranged for their convenience.

Now that two-income families are here to stay, raising the children is as much the responsibility of the partnership as is disposition of the paychecks.

It depends on your family members (their ages and proclivities)—when it comes to meal planning and preparation. It is tiresome to teach small children to cook and wash up after themselves. In the first place, they want to learn how to make only spaghetti and fudge and, as a rule, vegetable and salad fixing is rarely as popular as the pat-pat-patting of little round hamburgers. Attention spans and perspective are hard to learn. If you have patience and no other recourse, if you are gifted with farsightedness, you may be able on weekends to teach your children how to start the meals you or your husband will finish when one of you gets home from the office during the week. Remember, teaching someone in your family to cook is like teaching them to drive—you will probably go through a period of intense and mutual bitter hatred, so be ready for it. Expect lots of tears (including yours) and temper tantrums (including yours). The result, like having another grownup around who can drive, is worth the effort and heartache if you remember things will improve and your life will be easier than harder after a few months.

Older children tend to be arrogant in the kitchen because they feel *anybody* can cook (if *Mom* can) and so they go to the exotic dishes in the cookbook requiring forty-seven steps in the preparation and ingredients you don't have in the cupboard like cumin seed and curry. When such efforts end in disaster, and they always do, the cook retires in tears or extremes of disgruntlement to watch reruns of *Star Trek* and *The Mary Tyler Moore Show*, leaving the mess for someone else (you) to contend with or to eat. Teen-agers also feel put upon when they are asked to clean up the dinner dishes if they have prepared the dinner ("It's not fair!") and they and their fathers tend to leave far more pots, pans, beaters with hardened goo than you do, who know about cleaning up as you go along. They like to take short cuts—like using direct heat instead of a double boiler (even if using a double boiler is included in the all-important instructions) or putting the stove flame at high instead of low; often they tend to go off to chat on the phone for forty-five minutes while whatever it is burns away and the remaining mass has become the pot, left "to soak" for three weeks until you throw it out—the last remnant of your thirty-piece Revere Ware wedding present. Teenagers and husbands are hard to teach because they already *know*. Little children are hard to teach because while they are eager to learn, their motor coordination isn't very good and you have to tell them everything several times and then stand over them holding your breath while they attempt to do whatever is supposed to be done with a minimum of breakage or hilarious new ideas like spitting into the pot.

Don't feel inferior to women who talk or write Big Lie articles about how they've taught their children to willingly do all the housework and cooking, even down to scrubbing the woodwork and cleaning behind the toilet. It is difficult for me to swallow the idea of a cranky, pre- or post-adolescent child of eleven or fourteen cheerfully giving up his or her Saturdays to get down on the kitchen floor with a toothbrush along with equally spirited Mom and Dad and Sis, all singing in four part harmony as they labor to bring the interior of their house to spotless perfection. I'm not that gullible, nor are the members of my family more selfish or incompetent than others. I refuse to feel guilty or inferior because it turns out they hate housework as much as I do and attempt to avoid doing it with as much ingenuity as I do. If you think somebody else has talked their families into *cheerfully* taking on the communal responsibilities of a multimembered household, you are going to feel deeply intimidated. Tales about families with children who never complain and parents who are consistent, invariably cheerful, wise and energetic belong in *Ripley's Believe It or Not* and shouldn't be flaunted as possibilities for human beings. Use your common sense. Nobody likes housework, even those of us who were raised for it. Everybody is going to spend a lot of time grousing and complaining about the necessity of doing it, particularly when the work is parcelled out to everybody, instead of one main person who ends up in charge of all of it. When everyone understands they're all in it together, that life will improve in many ways if each carries his or her weight, then even cooperation between generations and sexes is possible.

Here are some good rules:

Be fair and accept the fact fairness is not always possible.

Demand fair treatment from others and accept the fact fairness is not always possible.

Avoid martyrdom: Don't do it all yourself.

Be flexible, willing to compromise, adjust and even change.
Listen, don't just tell.

Whatever works, keep. Whatever doesn't, get rid of (except blood relations, who should get a second chance).

CHAPTER SEVEN

Another Option: Entrepreneurship

AFTER YOU HAVE CONSIDERED THE VARIOUS DIMEN-sions of office work, it may be you decide you're not suited for it. Perhaps you are attracted to the freedom you have when you are your own boss. Because you cannot have maximum security and maximum freedom at the same time, you must decide whether you need security more than freedom, or vice versa, and then go in that direction.

Frankly, most people don't do well with unlimited freedom. They need boundaries and structure. They need rules. Often they need to work within a framework where these rules are imposed by others; most people also need the regular affirmation of a paycheck, as well as the safety of corporate numbers. When General Motors has a record loss for the year, no one person in the corporation is entirely to blame. There is reassurance in this mutual and numerous culpability. People get strength from each other. When a person who is in business for herself goes bust, there's no one else to blame. That's a lonely place to be. If she gets sick or goes out of town or loses interest in the undertaking, no one else is there to take up the slack. If the business is marginal, and most start-up businesses are for the first couple of years, the owner can never take a vacation, never side step the many responsibilities of that business. She must work very, very hard and she doesn't make much (if any) money those first twenty-five months or so.

Yet many people prefer to operate their own businesses despite the drawbacks. Don't ask me to explain the attraction. It is something ephemeral and seductive, that notion of running your own shop; it is part of what brought many of our ancestors to America and compelled their movement across the continent.

An entrepreneur not only organizes and administers a business venture; she also *assumes the risk for it.* You may enjoy organizing and operating projects, you may do it very well indeed, but taking the risk, personally, for the outcome of every project in which you are involved is strong medicine. A person who doesn't like to assume complete responsibility will not make a good entrepreneur (there's nobody around to blame). People who make excuses aren't likely entrepreneurs either, because customers don't care *why* you can't deliver, they care only that you do what you say you're going to do. You must be familiar with the flaws in your character as well as the strengths if you decide to go into business, because some flaws are good ones and some are disastrous when you're on your own.

Jeanne C., a chain-smoking, fast-talking energetic woman, told me early in our first session that although she'd "never done anything," she had considerable little-theater experience in suburban communities. She had participated by acting, directing, stage managing, and writing publicity.

She had been elected president of the theater group in the first suburban village she and her family had lived in, one where they moved a few years later and yet another on the occasion of her husband's most recent transfer. She had been elected president of all three groups shortly after joining each of them.

"Nobody else wanted to do it," she shrugged, scoffing at the importance of the position. "Everybody wants *to act.*

Nobody wants to do the work to get the plays on the boards and an audience in the seats."

"Did you want to act, too?" I asked.

"Certainly," came her response. "Why else would I join a little-theater group?"

Another reason for doing so might have been the chance to use her organizational skills.

As she talked about the kind of work she wanted to do, it became clear to both of us she had the kind of personality requiring a leadership role. Being a big fish was important to her: That's why she'd gone after those presidencies. She needed to be out front, making plans, assigning tasks, evaluating, jockeying people who didn't get along and nursing prima-donna complexes, being politically adroit, seeing the accounts were kept properly and goals were set, reached and new ones made. She was an effective executive. She had had primary responsibility for the management and production of over thirty plays in a ten-year period.

Her long-ago college degree had been in library science, hardly preparation for what she had ended up doing. Or so she thought at first.

We talked a long time about what the possibilities were for her in the job market. She admitted she was not certain how patient she could be, climbing the corporate ladder and waiting to be noticed and rewarded.

"I'm forty-seven years old," she commented. "I don't think I'm willing any more to be a go-fer."

She was fortunate and had some money, so her job search was not founded on desperation. She could afford to look around and do some deep thinking about the future she wanted to construct for herself. She finally decided she was best suited for running her own show. She made plans to start her own marketing research business, using the skills she had learned in college and those she had developed later as a manager and organizer.

She was lucky, not only because she clearly understood what she wanted, but she had the wherewithall to accomplish it. She could afford the experiment. She had wit, energy and understanding of the service she was offering.

She believed she could sell it to the people who needed it.

Yet she had told me during our first meeting she didn't know how to do anything.

Admittedly, Jeanne had a clear sense of mission and competence, once she gave herself a chance. Not many women or men have so much self-awareness, so much ability, and, let's face it, the good luck and the available dollars she had.

She was an ideal candidate for entrepreneurship.

Characteristics an entrepreneur must have include:

Energy

Resourcefulness

Commitment

Ability to withstand stress and criticism

Enthusiasm

Independence

Tenacity

If you are in charge, there will be nobody to run to, no one who can make the hard decision for you, no safety except that which you provide yourself. You will not be anybody's "little girl."

Does the possibility still excite you, thrill you, shoot you through with adrenaline? Read on.

Some businesses provide a product: potted plants, blouses and sweaters, scarves, desk blotters. Others provide services: catering, interior decorating, typing. You decide whether it is more logical for you to produce a product and sell it or whether what you want to do is more appropriately designed as a service you will provide to others.

People often say they are not the "creative type." For that reason, they believe it is impossible for them to have an idea. This is silly. You don't have to create an idea from the air. You construct a business idea step by step, just as you construct a resumé or make a pie. It is most likely someone else has had the idea for your business long before you came up with it. It may be your turn *to use* the idea. The importance is not whose idea it is, but whether or not it will fly *this* time. You can predict that by determining who has done it before you, how well they have done and how you feel about doing it, the amount of commitment you are ready to give the project.

Just because everybody has always said, "Oh, you're so good at giving dinner parties, you should go into the catering business" doesn't mean you should, especially if you've always hated giving dinner parties. Don't let *them* dictate to you. *To thine own self be true.* When you are an entrepreneur, self-knowledge is of maximum importance. If you don't enjoy whatever it is your business is involved with, you're up the creek. You will be spending eighteen hours a day doing it and thinking about it. Just imagine what those days will be like if you don't enjoy the exercise.

When you know what it is you want to do, no matter how bizarre, no matter how apparently useless or un-marketable you think it to be, define it in one declarative sentence. Make the sentence as simple and clear as you can. If you can't do that, you don't know what you're talking about yet. Go back to the drawing board and work on it until you are able to say exactly what it is you want to do:

I want to pot flowers and sell them.

I want to sew custom-made dresses.

I want to cater parties.

I want to find people who will be useful to other people (run an agency for domestic workers, tutors, baby-sitters).

This declarative sentence represents the idea for your business. You will work out a detailed "how it works," or operating plan later, as part of your business plan. (Don't be discouraged about all these "plans." When you are running your own show, you will see how easily and naturally each segues into the next.)

One of the ways you can get ideas of what other people are doing is by taking a look through your yellow pages. You will be amazed at the kinds of businesses people go into. Everything is listed there, (and often described fully in the ad copy) from Automatic Typewritten Letters to Mail

Order Wood Carving to Chartered Yachts. Ideas are not hard to come by; selection of which alternative is most appropriate for you is often the trouble spot.

You may think because nobody else has had your idea, it is new and untried and assured of success. This seems obvious to you because you can find nobody else who is doing it. You will have the market all to yourself and make bundles of money!

Beware of this conclusion. If nobody else is doing it, it probably means there's no money in it. Nobody wants it, nobody cares. Unless you are Henry Ford and you have come up with this decade's Model T, *seek competition.* The presence of competition most often means the product/ service has enough of a market so more than two or three separate businesses can make a go simultaneously. Now is not the time to live out the fantasy of publishing your own and friends' poetry, or to paint portraits of people on their own dinner plates. If other people aren't doing it, probably there is a good reason why they're not. The rare exception to this rule comes when you are able to identify coming movements in society and prepare some product or service responding to that shift and the new needs it produces. This is extremely iffy, but it can be done. It depends on your community and your proclivities. A few years ago some people read of the coming energy crisis, the burgeoning women's and consumer movements. They moved in, creating businesses to serve these new needs, and they did fine. More people failed than succeeded, though, even some of the most visionary, adventurous ones. Leave the ground-breaking to somebody else—unless you can afford to go bust. It is a good rule never to gamble more than you can afford to lose. Ninety-nine percent of the people who take avant-garde chances in new businesses fail. You want to succeed, so direct yourself to those areas which are proven, if undramatic, winners.

The Dollars

You will need money. In order to find out how much

money, you must sit down and figure out what your costs for one year will be. Costs include rent, telephone, office supplies and other material, equipment (purchased as well as rented), salaries (if any), insurance, taxes. Other costs which may be figured include advertising and marketing, postage, logo design, incorporation fees (if you decide to go that route), accountants and lawyers. You have to think of everything for which you will be billed. Stationery stores have spiral notebooks listing these items, to be used by small businesses. Buy one and use it.

One of the ways to make estimates of costs is to call up the appropriate vendors and ask them how much they charge for the things they offer.

When you decide how much money you're going to need, you must determine where you're going to find it. If the money is going to come from an outside-the-family source, it will be necessary to provide a business plan for the potential backer. That person will study it and decide whether you are a good risk or not. The document should be clear, thoughtful and complete. It doesn't have to be fancy. (Actually, you should write out such a plan even if you have the money for the enterprise yourself. It serves to organize your thinking, set priorities and will prevent you from going off on tangents during your first year.) Contents of a business plan include:

1. A summary definition of the product/service.
2. Your market. A description of who is likely to buy your product/service.
3. Your marketing plan. This describes how you propose to reach your market—direct mail, radio spots, newspaper ads, door-to-door, word of mouth, etc.
4. Your competition. Who else is doing it, how they are doing and why your idea is better or why it will succeed against the others.
5. Costs of running the business, including a breakdown of the production mechanics.
6. Biographical data. Use the resumé writing process, keeping in mind every sentence must be directed to the conclusion you are the best and most appropriate person to run this business.

One of the ways you can make sure you leave nothing out is to talk to other women who have gone into business for themselves in the last couple of years. You'll be surprised at how many of them there are. Ask them not only about their costs, but also what surprises, both good and bad, they've had, what they feel they were naive about, what they would change if they were going to do it again, what some of the pitfalls were. See if your town has an organization of small business owners. You should talk to women who have opened businesses, as well as men. Women will know better the pressures you are going to experience because of your sex.

If you are going to be owner and operator of your own business, you will find there are many people who have gone this route before you. Take advantage of their knowledge. Talk to them. Write to them. Read their books. Entrepreneurship is a trail with many markers.

Statistics to Ponder

Recently the U. S. Census Bureau published the findings of its survey on the *Selected Characteristics of Women-Owned Businesses*. Some of the findings include the following figures:

The median age of women business owners was 52.

Seventy-three percent of them were unmarried.

Almost 75 percent had some schooling beyond high school.

Eighty-six percent owned their business for the first time.

Over 70 percent of women-owned firms had no full- or part-time paid employees.

Forty-seven percent of the businesses were located at the owner's residence.

More than 60 percent were financed from the owner's savings.

Median net income for women-owned business was $6,481.

Over 80 percent were started with no capital or less than $10,000.

Forty-two percent of women-owned businesses had gross receipts of less than $5,000.

The ten industry groups accounting for the largest dollar volume of receipts for women-owned firms (in descending order) are:

Wholesale trade (non-durable goods);

Miscellaneous retail, eating and drinking places;

Wholesale trade (durable goods);

Food stores;

Automotive dealers and service stations;

Real estate;

Personal Services;

Apparel and accessory stores;

Special trade contractors.

The full study, *Women-Owned Business, 1977*, can be obtained from the Subscriber Services Section of the Bureau of the Census, Washington, D.C. 20233.

Since it is the most recent and most comprehensive information about businesses owned by women, it is a good idea to obtain a copy of it.

P & L

There are wonderful psychic benefits to running the show yourself. You will never feel so confident as when things are going well. It is heady and exhilarating.

On the other hand, there are things you will have to lay aside, probably permanently. No one will ever again perceive you as helpless. You will have to give up your unlimited ability to drop everything to serve someone else's needs. You may have to develop a thick skin; business owners have to make difficult, dollar-based decisions, often quickly and firmly. If you have a reputation for being a bleeding heart or a soft touch, you will have to give it up, at least for a while. Many people believe running your own business is part of the American Dream. Be prepared to handle their envy. You may be threatening to some people, people you had never imagined would be frightened by you. This may do damage to some of your relationships. Remember no relationship based on the incompetence or dependence of one of the participants is worth anything.

CHAPTER EIGHT

The New Pioneer

THE COMPETENCE YOU FEEL AND DEMONSTRATE WHEN you land a management job for yourself or when you open your business is a great feeling, but it doesn't come free. Stereotypes provide comfortable lap robes and shawls. You and the people around you never have a moment's doubt about what you're supposed to do when all the corners of your behavior are dictated by central casting. You can shout at the dinner table or run for the school board or pout in your room, but if you are unwilling to demonstrate your ability to participate in the man's world of making your living and paying your way (no matter what your marital status), you are accepting and perpetuating the stereotype role of woman as servant. Maybe you don't care . . . but some day your grandaughter might.

Because of inflation and the requirements brought about by the rising cost of living, the housewife stereotype is a myth anyway. Two income families are here to stay.

Yet still there is no such thing as a middle-class woman, because almost no woman is able to take care of herself by herself without slipping into the rigors of poverty. Most women we call middle-class require a man to provide for them because they and society believe they are not competent to contribute equally with men to the American economy. When they do, haphazardly, impermanently, fearfully, afraid of "unsexing" themselves, being "shrill," afraid of harming the fragile male ego, they are guaranteeing the inequities of the system will continue. We can't afford to be complacent about it.

When I married in 1956, almost every other woman my age was doing or trying to do the same thing. That was our section of the American Dream. Marriage, babies, a vine-covered center hall Colonial. Our husbands supported us as we made the nests.

Something has happened in the twenty-five years since then. Our daughters, young women coming out of schools and colleges, are not marrying so young. Or, if they are, they are putting off having babies and sometimes deciding not to have them altogether. They are afraid, quite legitimately, if they leave the work force they will never again be able to regain their places in it.

"Look at Mom," they say, pointing at us. "She's as well educated as Dad, she's as smart as he is, they love each other (maybe), but *she can't take care of herself.* All the money she has she must ask for from him. She is a permanent beggar. I don't want that to happen to me."

We must prove to our sons and daughters our lives have not been ruined, or our commitment unrewarded, because we chose to stay home from paid work to raise our families. We must show this was—and remains—a worthwhile choice. We must show that life experience outside a profit-making setting is valuable. Nobody else is going to recognize it if we don't. If we denigrate the skills we develop as managers of homes we invite others to join us in the put-down and we discover nobody will rescue us from our damaging self-assessment. One way we demonstrate the legitimacy of our accomplishments is when we transfer our skills to the world where people are paid for what they do. We don't ask for a free ride. Our skills are business-world real. They're administrative, organizational, developmental, motivational. We're qualified for the management jobs we seek. When we know our value, others will see we know it and soon they'll know it too. Being a housewife will be recognized as the skilled vocation it is—integral to the economy and as likely a place for responsible decision-making as anywhere on the conventional corporate ladder.

The choice we made when we decided to stay home to care for our families and provide unpaid services to our communities must be available to people of either sex as long as our society values the nuclear family. We mustn't allow the person who chooses this course to be punished when the children are grown, to find there is no place left anywhere except in the kitchen or behind a typewriter at a volunteer office or on a stool at the local saloon. We must make sure people have choices appropriate to their capability and ambition at the age of forty or fifty as well as at the age of twenty. Women who are over forty years old represent a resource of wisdom, experience and talent. When our competence is accepted, it will be easier for the ones who follow us to make the choices we made. Our obligation is not only to those who come after us, but to the women who preceded us and who—through their courage and tenacity—made participation in society outside our homes possible for us. I don't know many of the names of the women who fought for female suffrage and I don't know the names of the women who enrolled in colleges and universities when the popular opinion had it that thinking was physically harmful to women. Because of the actions of these brave women no one but me doubted my ability to perform without self-destruction when I decided to go to college. There was a place for me. What if I'd never had the chance?

The idea of American business welcoming middle-aged housewives into its mysteries is an unorthodox one, but when you think about it, the idea isn't any more unusual in our time than was the thought of Great Grandmother Hallie voting in hers. Like Hallie, we must prove our worth to earn a place. It won't be easy but she persevered and so must we. The battle is different but the objective is the same: to provide a legacy of opportunity for those who come after us.

We're the new pioneers. Let's get on with it.